Classroom Behaviour Management in Further, Adult and Vocational Education

Also available from Bloomsbury

Readings for Reflective Teaching in Further, Adult and Vocational Education,
    Margaret Gregson, Lawrence Nixon, Andrew Pollard and Trish Spedding
Reflective Teaching in Further, Adult and Vocational Education,
    Margaret Gregson and Yvonne Hillier
Teaching in Further Education, L.B. Curzon and Jonathan Tummons

Classroom Behaviour Management in Further, Adult and Vocational Education

Moving Beyond Control?

Edited by
Denise Robinson

BLOOMSBURY ACADEMIC
LONDON • NEW YORK • OXFORD • NEW DELHI • SYDNEY

BLOOMSBURY ACADEMIC
Bloomsbury Publishing Plc
50 Bedford Square, London, WC1B 3DP, UK
1385 Broadway, New York, NY 10018, USA

BLOOMSBURY, BLOOMSBURY ACADEMIC and the Diana logo are
trademarks of Bloomsbury Publishing Plc

First published in Great Britain 2019

A catalogue record for this book is available from the British Library.

A catalog record for this book is available from the Library of Congress.

ISBN: HB: 978-1-3500-7616-7
       PB: 978-1-3500-7615-0
       ePDF: 978-1-3500-7617-4
       eBook: 978-1-3500-7618-1

Typeset by Integra Software Services Pvt. Ltd.
Printed and bound in Great Britain

To find out more about our authors and books visit www.bloomsbury.com
and sign up for our newsletters.

Contents

Figures

Tables

Contributors

Editor

Denise Robinson is a consultant in education. She entered FE in 1975 moving into teacher education in 1987. She worked for FENTO/LLUK and was the director of a large teacher education partnership between the Huddersfield University Consortium and several FE colleges. She was awarded a National Teaching Fellowship by the HEA for her work in widening participation. Her interests are in teacher educator CPD. Her publications include 'Invisibility or Connecting Professionals?' in *Post-Compulsory Teacher Educators* (2016), co-editor of *Learning, Teaching and Development: Strategies for Action* (2015) and co-contributor to *Teaching in Lifelong Learning: A Guide to Theory and Practice* (2014).

Chapter contributors

Pete Bennett is Senior Lecturer in Post-Compulsory Education at the University of Wolverhampton, UK.

Pete spent twenty years teaching in an open-access sixth form college in the Black Country, during which time he co-authored and co-edited a range of textbooks and taught a range of subjects, including English Language and Literature, Communication Studies and Film. His research interests are broadly based across Cultural Studies, Critical Theory and Education, Teacher autonomy and Heavy Metal. He is the author/editor of a number of books, including *Popular Culture and the Myth of Austerity: Hard Times Today* (2016).

Joanne Irving-Walton is Principal Lecturer in Education in Initial Teacher Education at Teesside University, where she leads and manages an HEI-led Schools ITE partnership as well as a wider role within the university's Education Department.

Joanne has worked in education for seventeen years, beginning her career as a secondary English teacher in Newcastle-upon-Tyne. She went on to become a Head of English and a Local Authority English Advisor. She has responsibility for preparing for Ofsted inspections. In addition, she has experience of teaching abroad, within the private sector and at primary level. She has authored chapters in two textbooks.

Merv Lebor is a tutor in teacher education at the University Centre, Leeds City College; he has been a lecturer since 1975. He has taught from basic literacy up to Masters level and has much experience of dealing with disruptive students. He has led degree programmes, published numerous articles on education, arts and literature, including in the TES and in various journals. He has spoken at several conferences and published much on behaviour management; his latest book (2017) is *Classroom Behaviour Management in the Post-School Sector: Student and Teacher Perspectives on the Battle against Being Educated.*

Lou Mycroft works as an independent thinker, writer and educator with a background in public health and teacher education. She is an associate of the Education and Training Foundation and affiliated with the ET Consortium at the University of Huddersfield. She has pioneered pro-social approaches which build community both digitally and face-to-face. Lou would like to dedicate her chapter to Catina Barrett, 'Equalities in Education Campaigner and Force of Nature'. She has contributed chapters in *Teaching in Lifelong Learning* (2014), *Learning, Teaching and Development* (2015) and *Further Education and the Twelve Dancing Princesses* (2015).

Elizabeth Newton is Senior Lecturer in Teacher Education at the University Centre, Leeds City College, where she teaches on PGCE and Literacy/ESOL teacher training programmes.
    Elizabeth has taught in the secondary, FE and HE sectors since 1992. She has experience of teaching in France and Japan before returning to undertake postgraduate research. Elizabeth taught ESOL and EAP in the FE and HE sectors for ten years, working as a lecturer, course leader, mentor and learning leader. Recent conference papers include *Coaching for Sustainable Learning* (2016), Leeds Beckett University and *Autonomous Literacy Learners* – Sustainable Results International Conference, Birmingham.

David Powell is the Director of the University of Huddersfield Consortium, a HE–FE initial teacher education partnership with several FE colleges.
    David has worked in FE and HE since 1986. He has held various positions in teaching and management in a variety of institutions from small rural colleges to large city colleges. Since 2009 David has worked in HE. As part of this, he has managed various projects, including managing online learning activities to support the development of trainee teachers' subject specialist pedagogy and behaviour management within FE initial teacher education. Recent publications include *Practical Teaching* (2015).

Sandra Rennie is a teacher educator, consultant and education director for SEQUALS, an independent training provider based in Shipley, West Yorkshire. She has completed several action research projects on behaviour management in teacher education, equality and inclusion in FE and co-operative learning methods. Her approach is practice-based; starting from observed incidents and issues and working to develop alternative teaching and learning strategies through supported experimentation and reflection with colleagues. Recent publications include *Underneath the Observational Snapshot* (2015) and *Volunteer Teachers: Testing the Professionalisation Agenda in the Lifelong Learning Sector* (2012).

Joe Wearing is Course Leader in Teacher Education, University Centre, Leeds City College, UK, and works on Teacher Apprenticeships in both the Education and Training and school sector.

He has worked in education since 2002 first as an English teacher, including the Key Skills level 3 coordinator, and then second in department. He worked as CPD Lead involving the whole-school design and delivery of CPD. His interests are the role of coaching in developing teacher autonomy, the learner experience and improving aspiration in challenging schools. Joe has also taught at Leeds University as the PGCE English Lead.

Preface

Why has behaviour management in education received a higher profile than it did twenty-five years ago? Is it because students are more disruptive? Or because teachers report it more? Or because various government agencies such as Ofsted have deemed it to be an issue and, backed by behaviour consultant 'gurus', play on the preparedness of teachers who ensure compliance with Ofsted/government wishes? Teachers, as reconstituted 'classroom and learning managers', are no longer primarily there to teach but to manage future human resources; and students subconsciously or consciously recognize this. The teacher becomes not a trusted person but one who may change tack according to the whims of government diktat. Is the teacher working in the best interest of the individual student or to the latest policy directive? These may be the implicit concerns which emanate from this subtle but fundamental change in the teacher–student relationship contributing to 'bad' behaviour.

At the same time, despite flurries of policy activity and directives, the profile of the Further, Adult and Vocational Education sector (and that of their students and teachers?) remains low and is seen as second-best to an academic education. This may be regarded as a phenomenon rooted deep within the cultural psyche, structures and institutions of British society, clinging on to the last vestiges of class and empire. The mythology surrounding such a phenomenon has demonstrated its imperviousness to globalization. Despite inroads through the free-market system it persists and, it may be argued, has been strengthened and contributed to a rise in nationalism in many countries.

Yet for both students and teachers there are still opportunities to reclaim their true relationship, one which offers a bond between teacher and learner and one where both parties have authentic learning experiences. I hope this book will support this.

Denise Robinson

Foreword

JIM CRAWLEY

One key issue that all teachers and all teacher trainees regularly identify as central to their professional situation is how they can successfully work with their students to encourage good behaviour. Research also supports the idea that students' learning will be helped if challenging behaviour is reduced (Education Endowment Foundation 2018). The theme of this book will therefore be of interest to all. Its arrival will prove to be an important, comprehensive and most welcome addition to ITE and CPD programmes as it is based on well-argued ideas backed up by research and provides principles, examples, solutions and activities for behaviour management.

The book starts from a very important position, which is that good learning is most likely to take place in a positive and supportive environment, and that good behaviour is more likely when good learning is taking place. The highly experienced and well-respected team of practitioners and teacher educators who have produced this book emphasize that positive behaviour can come from a range of approaches, and that these are informed through and critically analysed by research.

The book begins with a consideration of the sector and societal context within which students are living, and how the life disruptions of students can contribute to disruptive behaviour in their learning situation. It continues to review and critique some of the current approaches which one could describe as on a continuum between compliance and control and motivation and learning-focused and considers how the values and life experiences of teachers can influence their own approaches to student behaviour.

The authors then introduce and discuss more a number of strategies in more detail, including affirmative mental health approaches; researching behaviour to inform practice and further research; drawing together 'expert tips' and reflection and trust in behaviour management.

Overall this book should be on every teacher's (and manager's) list of essential purchases.

Acknowledgements

This book could not have been written without the networks of teacher educators who exist across the UK. Their commitment to the students of their particular sector – be it the Education and Training (covering Further, Adult and Vocational Education and Training) or School sector – and their passion (here I use the word correctly and not merely as rhetoric) for learning and teaching have made this book possible.

While not all the contributors are from the Education and Training Consortium, University of Huddersfield, I would like to acknowledge the work of this partnership in supporting the provision and development for teacher educators across the network of FE Colleges and other associated institutions. Other contributors to this book are directly or indirectly connected to this partnership or one of the other teacher education partnerships around the country. They work tirelessly to promote a critically engaged profession of teacher educators. Long may it continue.

Abbreviations

ACL	Adult and Community Learning
ADHD	Attention Deficit and Hyperactive Disorder
AELP	Association of Employment and Learning Providers
CPD	Continuing Professional Development
DfE	Department for Education
DoH	Department of Health
ESOL	English for Speakers of Other Languages
ET	Education and Training
ETF	Education and Training Foundation
FBV	Fundamental British Values
FE	Further Education
FEFC	Further Education Funding Council
FENTO	Further Education National Training Organization
HE	Higher Education
LLUK	Lifelong Learning UK
MHFE	Mental Health in Further Education
NLP	Neuro Linguistic Programming
Ofsted	Office for Standards in Education
PKU	Professional Knowledge and Understanding
PRU	Pupil Referral Unit
PS	Professional Skills
PVA	Professional Values and Attributes
SEND	Special Educational Needs and Disability
UCU	University and College Union
UNESCO	United Nations Educational, Scientific and Cultural Organization
UTC	University Technical College
VET	Vocational Education and Training
WBL	Work-Based Learning

1 Introduction and Background to the Education and Training Sector

DENISE ROBINSON

The purpose of this book

> The extent of disruptive behaviour in the sector is wide and it is having an impact on the college image in general and recruitment, retention and achievement in particular.
> **MITCHELL ET AL. 1998: 23**

Such was the perception of behaviour in Further Education (FE) colleges in a research report published some twenty years ago by the FE Development Agency. Disruptive behaviour, as it was termed, was widespread due to social and economic changes with its consequential impact on individual students. More recently, the University and College Union (UCU) (2013) has identified similar behaviour with similar causes but now extending to those adult students required to attend courses to maintain their unemployment benefits. In addition, since 2015, all young people up to the age of eighteen are required to participate in some form of education, training or work with training (see DfE 2016). This has raised questions on student motivation (Wallace 2017) with its implications for behaviour. A similar scenario is presented regarding schools: 'We want to make sure that teachers have the necessary powers to maintain order in the classroom. It is unacceptable that poor pupil behaviour is the greatest concern of new teachers and a common reason why experienced teachers leave the profession' (DfE 2015).

This highlights the concern and the negative effects on teachers themselves of poor student behaviour. However, given the implementation of the 'Raising of the Participation Age' (DfE 2015), changes to the National Curriculum with a shift towards exam-focused 'rigour' and away from application, and anxiety expressed by students that vocational qualifications are perceived negatively (Atkins and Flint 2015: 5), there is a concern that an increasing number of students will become de-motivated. It has long been assumed that students in the Education and Training (ET) sector were present on a voluntary basis and clearly focused on achievement of qualifications for occupational and vocational careers. Yet, both ET and school teachers increasingly face disengaged, demotivated students and seek strategies to understand and connect with such students.

What is needed to support teachers and trainee teachers in their professional training and development is the provision of a text which provides a deeper, critical understanding alongside practical advice in managing behaviour when teaching students, whether this is in the wider learning and skills sector (sometimes referred to as either the ET or FE sector) or, indeed, for those students (14+) in schools, some of whom will progress into the ET sector. It is somewhat different to other texts on behaviour management in that it draws together teacher educators (all of whom are practitioner-researchers in the ET/Schools sectors) with a shared conviction of the need to engage trainee teachers in a dialogue of critical analysis in their developing professional practice. The intention is the development of the underpinning analytical capacity in trainees and teachers to apply appropriate strategies rather than merely a set of tools to apply in a mechanistic fashion.

This chapter acts as an introduction to the rationale for the book, its focus and its overarching theme. In doing this, it expounds an approach which supports trainees and teachers to analyse their contexts, students and roles in a meaningful way, leading to deeper understanding and applications that will bear fruit. It highlights the interplay between the range of public research and writings and that of practitioner research. This accentuates the role of practitioner research skills and application (as now demanded by professional bodies) and later chapters provide real examples of this. This does not diminish the value of published research; rather it makes the field of research more accessible, giving confidence to both trainees and teachers to explore issues such as behaviour through their own research and to share with other practitioners. Essentially, the approach is one of challenging a technicist approach which has a danger of reducing teaching to a set of formulae.

In this regard the book supports the aspirational approach of the Education and Training Foundation (ETF), the Department for Education (DfE) Professional Development standards and the Higher-Level Apprenticeship in Teaching and Learning. Furthermore, it supports the growing number of trainee teachers in the ET sector who, increasingly, request teaching experience in the Schools sector, mainly in the vocational subjects for 14+ students. This underlines the need to be aware of the various comparisons between schools and the ET sector and is addressed to a limited extent throughout this book.

The focus is not on 'deviant' students or those who have been excluded and moved to Pupil Referral Units. It is, rather, on what might be referred to as 'standard' students and standard learning situations. The term 'standard' belies the reality of teaching; there is no one standard student, class, institution or environment. However, the experience of teachers of a seemingly underlying phenomenon leads to an exploration of issues that goes beyond hints and tips (although these are useful) and even sophisticated strategies and prompts questions about the deeper condition of society.

But what do we mean by 'bad' behaviour? As cited earlier this might be referred to as 'disruptive' behaviour meaning almost any behaviour which leads to a distraction or disturbance which interferes with learning. This might include chatting, ignoring the teacher, or reading messages on mobile phones at one end of the spectrum, with more extreme examples such as swearing, challenging the teacher's authority, racist/sexist abuse and even physical threats or acts at the other end. The age of the student is not a determining factor; 'bad' behaviour can be displayed by adults as well as younger teenagers. Examples of these behaviours will be found in various chapters in this book.

Backdrop to the sector

The ET sector is a large, complex but low-profile sector. Sometimes referred to as the 'Cinderella service' (Randle and Brady 1997), although it makes certain 'star' appearances in government policy, these tend to be one-offs with the media and the population at large having little interest in them. Yet it continues to educate many more people than in the other education sectors. To understand the environment in which the sector is operating and its potential impact on participants, the following statistics and comments may be useful. Note that statistics are difficult to gather not only because of the complexity of the ET sector but also as responses for data collection are given to the ETF on a voluntary basis. The focus of most publications tends to be on English provision although the ETF does collect data for all four nations of the UK.

Institutions

- There are around 1,150 publicly funded FE providers in England delivering learning to around 4 million learners.
- There are 273 FE colleges (including 64 Sixth Form Colleges) in England with twenty in Scotland and thirteen in Wales.

Students

- FE colleges educate and train 2.2 million people in England alone in colleges, Adult and Community Learning (ACL) and Work-Based Learning (WBL) (AoC 2017); Wales has 172,470 equivalent students (Welsh Government 2018) with 22,000 in Scotland (Auditor Scotland 2017). This compares to the 1,563,900 18-year-old students undertaking degrees in universities in 2016 of whom 10.6 per cent were from low-participation areas (UUK 2017).
- There are 773,000 (37 per cent) of 16–18-year-olds in colleges, compared with 442,000 (22 per cent) in schools (AoC 2017).
- There are 313,000 people undertaking apprenticeships through colleges (AoC 2017).
- There are 16,000 14–15-year-olds enrolled at FE colleges (AoC 2017).
- Around 150,000 students are studying at HE level in colleges (AoC 2017).

Policies and agencies

There is a long history of what has been referred to as 'benign neglect' (Lucas 2004) in terms of policy-attention to FE colleges and the wider sector. This appeared to change from the 1980s when the introduction of 'initiatives' such as the Technical and Vocational Educational Initiative proliferated and, later, greater interest in policy from the New Labour government (1997–2010) with the introduction of various quangos (such as the FE National Training Organization and the Standards Unit) which sought to improve standards through direct intervention and regulation. The approach changed with the coalition government's (2010–2015) position as stated by John Hayes, the then skills minister, that, for example, it was 'crucial' that the new Education and Training Foundation should be 'truly of the sector, by the sector and for the sector' (Hayes 2012). Despite such policy moves (including the deregulation of the requirement for teachers in the ET sector to be teacher qualified), policy direction continued. The present government has promised a new industrial strategy which indicates a return to greater state intervention. In February 2018, the prime minister announced a review of post-18 education and training, declaring that she wanted to 'give every young person access to an education that suits their skills and aspirations' and repeating from an earlier position (May 2016) that she wanted 'to make Britain a Great Meritocracy'.

There are several problems here. There have been numerous prime ministers and others who have announced reviews of vocational education, decrying its low esteem and identifying how the country needs to improve its vocational education and training if it is to maintain its economic position and competitiveness. This dates to the early nineteenth century when the government realized that other countries (and particularly Germany) were seemingly making great strides forward in their economies and that their vocational education and training (VET) systems were supporting such improvements. Policy initiatives have each been given a fanfare as the way to improve VET and raise its profile as a genuine alternative route to academic and university education. Over the last thirty years much has been said about 'parity of esteem' between vocational and academic study and qualifications but it has proved to be a chimera. Why should this seem to be so difficult to achieve? Hyland (2010) suggests that such objectives 'present a fundamental challenge to the deep-seated prejudice and negative valuing of vocationalism that is endemic in the system' and that until this abates it will continue to be difficult to improve the standing of vocational qualifications. Indeed, there has been further questioning of the 'parity of esteem' in research undertaken by Shields and Masardo (2017) which contends that students entering university degree courses with vocational qualifications are less likely to achieve a first- or upper second-class degree.

Furthermore, the aspiration of achieving a 'Great Meritocracy' may be a misunderstanding of the notion of meritocracy. The term was first coined by Michael Young in 1958 but was projected as a dystopian scenario where those of intellect and academic qualifications would become a new, dominant class. A meritocracy will lead to some winners, having greater opportunities to climb the social ladder, but many 'left-behinds'. The other side of upward social mobility is, of course, downward social mobility, so rather than promote meritocracy, it is suggested that the focus for improvement should be across the board social equality that improves the lot of all (see the Social Mobility Commission's report 2017). The report states: 'Britain is a deeply divided nation' and highlights under-investment in areas of deprivation (rural and coastal areas, old industrial areas, for example).

The sector has been subjected to policy churn and an ever-changing set of agencies and ministers (Norris and Adam 2017). Thus:

- According to the Institute for Government (2017), since the 1980s there have been twenty-eight major pieces of legislation, forty-eight secretaries of state with relevant responsibilities, and no organization has survived longer than a decade. There have been at least two industrial strategies in the last decade alone – and we are now moving onto a third.

- In the three decades up to the 2015 general election there had been sixty-one secretaries of state responsible for skills policy in Britain. Between them they produced thirteen major Acts of Parliament and skills policy had flipped between government departments or been shared between departments on ten different occasions (City and Guilds 2014: 1).

- 'My opening remark to Principals of FECs was always – "I speak to you a few months before the opening of the LSC [Learning and Skills Council], and a few short years before it closes." This cynical view of education quangos was indeed borne out. Although the Further Education Funding Council (FEFC), created as a result of the Further and Higher Education Act of 1992, lasted for nine years, the LSC bumped along for seven, and there has been an alphabet soup of no less than six successor bodies to the FEFC over the last 16 years' (David Melville 2018, reflecting on his role as CEO for the FEFC, 1996–2001).

Apprenticeships

More recently, one policy area of VET has received a much higher profile compared to previous years. Apprenticeships have a long history dating back to 1563 but came to their peak in the 1960s with one-third of all boys leaving school to become apprentices (Mirza-Davies 2015). Decline in numbers and their perceived utility to employment practices and expectations led to reforms to improve the standards and employer requirements. The Conservative government (2017) pledged a target of 3 million apprentices by 2020. However, these latest reforms seem to be experiencing problems. The target for the numbers of apprentices fell short by 61 per cent in 2017 compared to the same period for 2016 and in its first inspection of providers a report by Ofsted March 2018 stated: 'Apprenticeships are "not fit for purpose"' (Ryan 2018). Furthermore, the ETF, established by the coalition government in 2012, appears to be in some disarray given the withdrawal of the Association of Employment and Learning Providers (AELP) from the Board of the ETF in March 2018. Given the government's policy of improving social mobility via the provision of lower-level apprenticeships, the question arises as to how this may impact on perceptions of opportunity on the part of those families seeking prospects for their children. Furthermore, evidence of VET's lack of parity with academic qualifications is provided in research on student perceptions where students from lower social grades are more likely to study vocational qualifications than academic Advanced (A) levels (UCU 2014) and 'perceived attractiveness of VET was closely associated with societal perception of their programmes (which the young people considered to be negative)' (Atkins and Flint 2015: 5).

Comparing the Education and Training sector with the School sector

The trainee or teacher may now find her/himself expected to experience both sectors and, indeed, may be looking to work across both sectors. While there are matters that differentiate students across the two sectors, there are many others that conjoin them; understanding the social, economic and social contexts is key. Knowing something of the commonalities, contrasts and challenges of each sector which feature in the backdrop to an understanding of behavioural issues is important. Here are some basic indicators of the differences between the two sectors.

- The focus on academic students does not seem to be purely a present phenomenon. In 1959, the Crowther Report stated: 'There is a tendency of long historical standing in English educational thought (it is not nearly so visible in some other countries) to concentrate too much on the interests of the abler pupils in any group that is being considered and to forget about the rest' (Crowther 1959).

- Student funding is lower in the ETF sector. 'The 22% lower funding per student for 16–19-year-olds than for 11–16-year-olds has no logic and results in tough decisions being made about the curriculum offer, breadth of learning and support which students receive' (Hughes 2017).

- Teachers are paid on average less than schools teachers and their working hours and conditions of service are very different (e.g. teachers in FE colleges will be expected to work evenings and their holidays are less than school teachers). The average salary for FE teachers in 2015–2016 was £30,288. It was £37,400 for school teachers and £25,389 in independent training providers (ETF 2017: 30).

- There were around 326,000 staff in the ET sector and this is declining by around 3 per cent each year. There is a total of 1.4 million staff in the Schools sector with around 503,000 full-time teachers.

- The average age of teaching staff is forty-six in colleges but slightly lower in training organizations where 60 per cent are under forty-five. For secondary schools the average age is thirty-nine years (Cambridge Assessment 2017).

- In the ET sector, most teaching staff (around 75 per cent) hold a teaching qualification. In the Schools sector, all teachers are required to hold a teaching qualification (other than free schools).
- Over 60 per cent of teachers in colleges report undertaking no Continuing Professional Development (CPD) (Greatbatch and Tate 2018). Staff in schools are required to undertake CPD.
- The range of curricula and qualifications is vastly different. The Schools sector is obliged to follow the National Curriculum with some notable exceptions. The ET sector has something like 13,000 technical qualifications, in addition to a range of Advanced level qualifications, professional qualifications and other short courses.
- State schools have, since 2002, developed various institutional structures through the introduction of academy schools and free schools, university technical colleges (UTCs) and studio schools. They are all independent of the local education authority receiving funding directly from central government and from sponsors. Gillard (2007) has reported on the early years of the academies, including the reduction (and, ultimately, ending) of local education authority controls, elements of privatization through business-based controls and consultant contracts for marketing as one example, and the use of these changes to include selection (e.g. based on a specialized curriculum or religion). The ET sector is vast in terms of its institutions, colleges (general, sixth form and specialist), adult and community learning, private training organizations and prison learning. Funding for ET is also complex with various agencies, student fees and employer contributions in the ever-changing mix.

Behaviour

The above has set the scene for behaviour management in terms of policies, the complexities of the sector, and the staff and students who inhabit this environment. The backdrop of policy formation can be viewed from a perspective of risk aversion which, according to Beck (2000), is the lot of the modern world and is predicated essentially on globalization with its destabilization effect, particularly on traditional ways of working and thinking. It has been asserted that all education sectors are affected as 'the overwhelming emphasis today is on individualism, materialism, consumption and personal acquisition' (Smyth 2011: 3). In a world where relationships are increasingly determined by such values and impose themselves in the classroom, addressing behavioural issues as an adjunct to this is likely to lead to failure. The notion that students are there to be merely trained as the future work force will likely alienate students and staff. Yet there is overt focus on the business model where financial targets (often linked to student achievement of specific qualifications) may, even if inadvertently, place student learning in a secondary role (see Chapter 2 for further development of this). Writers such as Giroux (2011) assert that teachers and students should actively transform knowledge rather than merely consume it and that education should aim at 'producing citizens who are critical, self-reflective, knowledgeable, and willing to make moral judgements and act in a socially responsible way' (2011: 3). This, we may think, is indeed a worthy aim but how can we achieve this? Jardine (2012) refers to creating spaces where teachers can fulfil their true role as teachers, rather than mere technicians applying the latest policy or strategy. Teachers should be intellectuals or producers of theories (see Smyth 2011) and this is where teachers should and can operate as practitioner/researcher. Chapters 5, 6 and 7 offer specific examples of practitioner research in behaviour.

However, there are some aspects of behaviour which seem to present themselves as being more prevalent over the last twenty years or so and that is mental health. Over the last two decades there has been increasing expansion of regulation as well as responsibility for the physical aspects of health and safety to one which encompasses 'well-being', including mental health. Although teachers have a responsibility for the health and well-being of their students, there has developed, according to Ecclestone and Hayes (2009), a tendency to regard students as vulnerable with a resulting focus on protection. Some have argued that this has had a pathologizing result. Ball et al. (2011) argue that 'behaviour policy, like other policies, is enacted in particular and distinct institutional contexts with their own histories; that behaviour policy at the [school] level is an ensemble of issues/fragments, principles, directives/imperatives and procedures/practices which are messy and complex; and that behaviour policy is very much a collective enterprise'. While this refers to schools, readers may identify the issues as applicable to many other institutional contexts. While it is easier to find studies on mental health in higher education (see, for example, Storrie et al. 2010), Buchanan (2013) has undertaken research on adult students in the FE sector. The question is why have mental health issues become such a problem? Is this a matter of reporting or is it an indicator of something much more profoundly disturbing about the alienation of young people from their sense of purpose in a highly commercialized society?

Direct regulations from government on behaviour are not evident for the ET sector and although the sector may experience a seeming 'hands-off' approach to policy in this field, Ofsted expectations (see *FE and Skills Inspection Handbook* (Ofsted 2018), section on personal development, behaviour and welfare) tend to govern the approach to behaviour management. The grade descriptors offered are intended to influence, if not determine, institutional practices. The Association of Colleges (AoC) and the UCU both offer guidance, often informed by research (see, for example, *Whole College Behaviour Management: Final Report*; UCU 2013).

This book is not about managing 'disaffected' students as such but giving an insight on behaviour through a critical 'eye' and, drawn from the experience of the authors, as to how practitioners can both understand and relate to professional standards and their application, both for initial teacher training and for CPD. This reflects an underlying concern with a focus on the individual as opposed to social issues: 'Constructing problems as individual deficits also obscures the class, race and gender blindness of curricula and hence wider understandings of how power is exercised and in whose interests' (Smyth 2011: 36).

The chapters

While addressing the needs of trainee teachers and practitioners, this book recognizes the range of courses and their different levels, including level 4 (such as Diplomas in Education for those in FE) to levels 6 and 7 (Masters incorporated into Post Graduate Certificates) being undertaken by trainees and practitioners. Thus, some chapters may be perceived to be at different levels. This presents opportunities: stretching some trainees to achieve their potential; offering a range of approaches and 'levels' on this demanding and highly complex aspect of teacher training/education; and it offers CPD for teachers to refresh and develop their practice in this field.

Chapter 2 addresses, within a critical theoretical context, what lies beneath these discussions about 'managing behaviour'. What are the implications of thinking in terms of 'classroom management' and thus 'classroom managers' rather than 'teaching' and 'teachers', particularly in the context of the 'neo-liberal turn' within the dominant economies of the world (and particularly the UK and United States). Using Foucault's genealogical approach Bennett provides an 'untidy' history of our present situation which combines elements of policy, philosophy, autobiography and practice. Bennett presents arguments about the context in which students exist and how these might present a different perspective on students and their behaviour. Are some students (and, indeed, staff) facing essential contradictions within their experience of education and training that offers them little opportunity for life's fulfilments and divides them ultimately from their own learning? Is there any hope for emancipating the so-called learner if we cannot first emancipate their teachers?

In Chapter 3 Lebor explores the language used to describe practice in the classroom: Which words do we use to describe negative situations? What happens when behaviour is overwhelmingly negative and the teacher feels as if they are in highly conflicted environments? Lebor examines different versions of the language of behaviour management and explores different ways of envisioning classrooms in post-school contexts. His work looks at the complexities and contexts of violence relevant to educational settings and suggests a range of strategies that can be used to counter disruptive behaviours in classrooms. The author looks at the attitudes and concerns of a range of teachers, trainers and theorists. How students are constructed by teachers, but also the behavioural consequences of different models of being a teacher are crucial to this chapter. This will be used to contrast and show some crucial differences between schools and post-school contexts.

Chapter 4 offers a range of behavioural management approaches as applied to a range of learning contexts and critique. Rennie includes a description and critique of 'tough love' and liberal approaches and those approaches informed by practitioner research. Teachers' own experience of being a learner are referenced, including their personal expectations of behaviour standards. How do differences in cultural background, status and social position influence the relationships between teachers and learners? The learning provider's ethos, culture and organizational stability and how these impact on the behaviour of teachers and learners is addressed. Why do some teachers adopt a particular approach and what may change this? What is an effective counter-strategy to such approaches?

Chapter 5 gives a perspective on mental health issues and how these may be a critical component of some of the behavioural issues students display and which are observed in the learning environment. Many teachers (and especially trainees) express concern about their lack of understanding of mental health issues and how it might affect the behaviour of their students. While Mycroft does not offer clinical strategies for dealing with such behaviour, she draws on the emerging philosophy of neurodiversity to offer practical, realistic strategies for trainees, teachers and trainers. By highlighting how mental health can impact on behaviour, trainees and teachers can increase their awareness and confidence to enable them to respond positively. The chapter incorporates Mycroft's involvement in a national practitioner training project on mental health in education and her considerable experience in the field of professional development.

Chapter 6 provides an overview of further education-based research undertaken into behavioural issues as well as expounding the need for teacher research. It considers Robert Marzano's evidence-based practice research into classroom management and asks what might be learned from it in terms of classroom management and possible future institutional-based research. To provide examples of such approaches to research, Powell critically reviews three pieces of FE-based research and finally considers three methodologies (action research, self-study and living theory) that offer trainee teachers, teachers and their students, and teacher educators collaborative and socially just approaches to research that seek to gain a deeper understanding of what lies behind behavioural issues to develop democratic and humane solutions for all. Although focused on FE, the research-practitioner approach is applicable to the Schools sector.

Chapter 7 explores a selected range of strategies (among a myriad of strategies) to use to improve behaviour in the place of learning and how these could help teachers develop strategies for establishing stability in a chaotic situation. It demonstrates how to use supported experimentation to tackle personally challenging behaviour. Rennie includes various approaches including breaking out of entrenched and repetitive behaviour patterns through improvisation and creative actions; identifying and responding to non- verbal cues; and using drama and role play to build up a repertoire of scripts and actions for redirecting unproductive behaviour. The chapter aims to showcase one application of a theory to practise and present a model of teachers thinking for themselves.

In Chapter 8 Newton and Robinson explore a range of reflective models, from the seminal works of Schon's (1983, 1987) 'reflection in action', through to Tripp's (1993) 'critical incident analysis' and Brookfield's (1995) 'critical reflection'. These models include how values and structural issues can affect teaching and learning. It describes an approach identified as 'restorative conversations' between students and teachers and how it has been used on one FE college. Above all, trust is regarded as a constant feature of good behaviour management.

Chapter 9 considers how the behaviour management strategies employed by individual teachers are shaped and guided by the wider ethos and approach of whole institution systems and how teachers and their students develop their approach to behaviour through interaction with these systems and the ethos. It contextualizes the role of the teacher within the wider behaviour management structures of schools and colleges and their professional partnerships and explores the role of behaviour within the teachers' standards, ongoing CPD and within the inspection frameworks (noting that the standards in the compulsory sector are distinct from those that apply in the post-compulsory sector). The impact of successive policy changes on the way in which behaviour management is framed within education is considered as are popular perspectives and attitudes and their role in guiding the approach of institutions. Irving-Walton provides vignettes of different institutions providing an insight into diverse ways of working. Differing internal structures for the management of behaviour are considered alongside the effect of varying institutional types.

Chapter 10 considers the three areas of the updated ETF Professional Standards: professional skills, professional values and attributes, and professional knowledge and understanding. It demonstrates how the different standards can be used to improve professional understanding and application to behaviour management. What does Ofsted say about behaviour? While elements of the professional standards may be aspirational, a targeted approach to a specific issue such as behaviour can help realize those aspirations.

In conclusion to this introduction, we can see that if the 'belief that if we only select the right standardized procedures, enacted the right institutional structures, get the right funding, forms and assessment regimes, and so on, teachers' and students' futures will be finally secured and assured and peace will reign' (Jardine 2012: 3), there will surely be problems ahead. Rather what is needed is a critical approach in our understanding of the nature of society and how this impacts on our students and their behaviour. This is not a pessimistic view but one which, based on our knowledge, skills and experience, seeks to address the issues and offers approaches which will enable our students to grow and realize their potential for self-fulfilment.

Activities

1 Consider the behavioural policy of the institution in which you work or train. What values and expectations are reflected in the policy? How does it incorporate Ofsted grade descriptors for behaviour?

2 What ET institutions can be found in your region? What role or purpose do they serve? Now consider the range of schools for students from 14+. Are there any overlaps in curriculum offers or in ethos that compare to those in the ET institutions?

3 How might an awareness of critical approaches to pedagogy inform your understanding of behavioural issues?

Further reading

Kellner, D. (2003), 'Toward a Critical Theory of Education', *Democracy and Nature*, 9 (1): 51–64.
This paper provides a useful overview of education philosophy from the Greeks and Romans through to the present day, emphasizing the position and development of critical pedagogy. Kellner offers a view on how education should be developed in today's globalized world to give young people education to respond to the social, technological, economic and ecological challenges they will face.

Norris, E. (2017), *Further Education Policy Gets Churned to Death*. Yorkshire Post, 16 March.
Available at: https://www.yorkshirepost.co.uk/news/opinion/emma-norris-further-education-policy-gets-churned-to-death-1-8440728.
This article considers the consequences of policy churn in the FE sector, drawing from the Institute of Government's statement/paper (2017).

Richardson, W., and Wiborg, S. (2010), *English Technical and Vocational Education in Historical and Comparative Perspective: Considerations for University Technical Colleges*. Baker Dearing Educational Trust.
This report, along with recommendations for the newly created University Technical Colleges, provides a useful historical overview (including international comparisons) of the development of technical and vocational education and training from 1880.

References

AoC (2017), *College Key Facts 2017–18*, London: AoC.

Atkins, L., and Flint, K.J. (2015), 'Nothing Changes: Perceptions of Vocational Education in England', *International Journal of Training Research*, 13 (1): 35–48.

Auditor General (2017), *Scotland's Colleges 2017*, Audit Scotland.

Ball, S., Hoskins, K., Maguire, M., and Braun, A. (2011), 'Disciplinary Texts: A Policy Analysis of National and Local Behaviour Policies', *Critical Studies in Education*, 52(1): 1-14.

Beck, U. (2000), *What Is Globalization?*, Cambridge: Polity.

Brookfield, S. (1995), *Becoming a Critically Reflective Teacher*, 1st edn, San Francisco, CA: Jossey-Bass.

Buchanan, D. (2013), 'A Phenomenological Study Highlighting the Voices of Students with Mental Health Difficulties Concerning Barriers to Classroom Learning', *Journal of Further and Higher Education*, 38 (3): 361–376.

Cambridge Assessment (2017), *The Average Age of Teachers in Secondary Schools*, Cambridge: Cambridge Assessment.

City and Guilds (2014), *Sense and Instability: Three Decades of of Skills and Employment Policy*, London: City and Guilds.

Crowther, G. (1959), *A Report of the Central Advisory Council for Education (England)*, London: The Stationery Office.

Department for Education (2015), *Policy Paper. 2010–2015 Government Policy: School Behaviour and Attendance*, London: DfE.

Department for Education (2016), *Participation of Young People in Education, Employment or Training*. Available online: https://assets.publishing.service.gov.uk/government/uploads/system/uploads/attachment_data/file/561546/Participation-of-young-people-in-education-employment-or-training.pdf (accessed 23 April 2018).

Ecclestone, K., and Hayes, D.(2009), *The Dangerous Rise of Therapeutic Education*, Abingdon, Oxon: Routledge.

ETF (2017), 'Further Education Workforce Data for England. Analysis of the 2015–2016 Staff Individualised Record (SIR) Data', *Frontier Economics*. ETF, 2017.

Mitchell, C., Pride, D., Howard, L., and Pride, B. (1998), *Ain't Misbehavin*, Further Education Development Agency. Available online: https://eric.ed.gov/?id=ED421654 (accessed 15 February 2018).

Gillard, D. (2007), 'Axes to Grind: The First Five Years of Blair's Academies', *Education in England*. Available online: www.educationengland.org.uk/articles/25academies.html (accessed 25 March 2018).

Giroux, H.A. (2011), *On Critical Pedagogy*, London: Bloomsbury.

Greatbatch, D., and Tate, S. (2018), *Teaching, Leadership and Governance in Further Education*, London: DfE.

Hayes, J. (2012), 'Foreword', in *Developing a Guild for Further Education*, London: DBIS.

Hughes, D. (2017), *AoC Responds to Ofsted's Annual Report*. Available online: https://www.aoc.co.uk/news/aoc-responds-ofsted's-annual-report (accessed 14 March 2018).

Hyland, T. (2010), 'On the Upgrading of Vocational Studies: Analysing Prejudice and Subordination in English Education', *Educational Review*, 54 (3): 287–296.

Jardine, D.W. (2012), *Pedagogy Left in Peace: Cultivating Free Spaces in Teaching and Learning*, New York: Continuum.

Lucas, N. (2004), 'The "FENTO Fandango": National Standards, Compulsory Teaching Qualifications and the Growing Regulation of FE College Teachers', *Journal of Further and Higher Education*, 28 (1): 35–51.

May, T. (2016), *Britain, the Great Meritocracy: Prime Minister's Speech*, DfE, PM's Office, 9 September. Available online: https://www.gov.uk/government/speeches/britain-the-great-meritocracy-prime-ministers-speech (accessed 12 March 2018).

Melville, D. (2018), *We're Likely to Miss HEFCE More Than We Know*, WONKHE, 19 March. Available online: https://wonkhe.com/blogs/were-likely-to-be-miss-hefce-more-than-we-know/?utm_medium=email&utm_campaign=Monday%20Morning%20HE%20Briefing%20-%2019th%20Mar (accessed 12 May 2018).

Mirza-Davies, J. (2015), *A Short History of Apprenticeships in England: From Medieval Craft Guilds to the Twenty-First Century*, London: House of Commons Library.

Norris, E., and Adam, R. (2017), *All Change. Why Britain Is So Prone to Policy Reinvention, and What Can Be Done About It*, London: Institute for Government.

Ofsted (2018), *FE and Skills Inspection Handbook*, Ofsted: Crown Copyright.

Randle, K., and Brady, N. (1997), 'Managerialism and Professionalism in the "Cinderella Service"', *Journal of Vocational Education and Training*, 49 (1): 121–139.

Ryan, G. (2018), 'Apprenticeships "Not Fit for Purpose" at First Provider Visit in Ofsted Focus on New Training Providers', *TES FE Focus*, 15 March. Available online: https://www.tes.com/news/further-education/breaking-news/apprenticeships-not-fit-purpose-first-provider-visited-ofsted (accessed 28 March 2018).

Schon, D. (1983), *The Reflective Practitioner: How Professionals Think in Action*, London: Temple Smith.

Schon, D. A. (1987), *Educating the Reflective Practitioner: Toward a New Design for Teaching and Learning in the Professions*, San Francisco, CA: Jossey-Bass.

Shields, R., and Masardo, A. (2017), 'False Equivalence? Differences in the Post-16 Qualifications Market and Outcomes in Higher Education', *Educational Review*, 70 (2): 149–166.

Smyth, J. (2011), *Critical Pedagogy for Social Justice*, New York: Continuum.

Social Mobility Commission (2017), *State of the Nation 2017: Social Mobility in Great Britain*, London: Crown Copyright.

StatsWales (2017), *Provider Learners Enrolled at Further Education and Higher Level Institutions Excluding Higher Education Learning Programmes*. Available online: https://statswales.gov.wales/Catalogue/Education-and-Skills/Post-16-Education-and-Training/Further-Education-and-Work-Based-Learning/Learners/Further-Education/providerlearnersenrolledfurthereducationhighereducationinstitutions

Storrie, K., Ahern, K., and Tuckett, A. (2010), 'A Systematic Review: Students with Mental Health Problems – A Growing Problem', *International Journal of Nursing Practice*, 16: 1–6.

Tripp, D. (1993), *Critical Incidents in Teaching. Abingdon*, Oxon: Routledge.

Universities UK (2017), *Patterns and Trends in UK Higher Education 2017*, London: UUK.

UCU (2013), *Classroom Management: UCU Continuing Professional Development*. Available online: http://cpd.web.ucu.org.uk/files/2013/07/CPD-factsheet-6.pdf

UCU (2014), *Young People's Perceptions About Post18 Education and Training Options*, London: UCU.

Wallace, S. (2017), *Adult Education*, Exeter: Learning Matters.

Welsh Government (2018), *Further Education, Work-Based Learning and Community Learning*. Available online: http://gov.wales/statistics-and-research/further-education-work-based-learning-community-learning/?lang=en

Young, M. (2017) [1958], *The Rise of the Meritocracy*, London: Routledge. Previously published by Thames and Hudson.

2 Why We Must Never Become Classroom Managers

PETE BENNETT

Introduction

This chapter offers a genealogical account of the issues surrounding 'classroom management' as manifest in schools, in the Education and Training sector and in Teacher Education departments. Genealogy here is one of Foucault's (1926–1984) methodological 'weapons' for flushing out assumptions, claims about what is right and what is wrong, and judgements based on second-order political positions. It does not believe that history is going somewhere or indeed has come from anywhere, but it does seek to identify the contingent events which may have prompted one course of action over other possibilities (Kendall and Wickham 1999: 29–31). In 2014 Ofsted published a report, *Low-level Disruption in Classrooms: Below the Radar*, which underlined the degree to which a neo-liberal and at the same time retrogressive agenda had gripped English education. This 'survey report looking into the nature and extent of low-level disruptive behaviour in primary and secondary schools in England' was widely reported with the headlines suggesting that 'pupils are potentially losing up to an hour of learning each day in English schools because of this kind of disruption in classrooms' (Ofsted 2014: 5). Although this focuses on schools it has much to say to ET institutions as well.

The idea that such a crude, unproblematized model of learning (which assumes 'listening' and 'learning' are synonymous) should be deployed is reason enough for response, but both the methodology and the more detailed findings also expose the need for a more significant critique. There was also no recourse to a right to reply for the so-called learners whose 'disruptions' these apparently were, so this will hopefully be provided here as well. The report claimed to draw on 'evidence from Ofsted's inspections of nearly 3,000 maintained schools and academies' including 'from 28 unannounced inspections of schools where behaviour was previously judged to require improvement' (Ofsted 2014: 4). More problematically still the report is supplemented by two surveys 'conducted independently by YouGov, gathering the views of parents and teachers' (Ofsted 2014).

One thing that Ofsted and I both agree on is that 'the findings set out in this report are deeply worrying', though for very different reasons. The big news of this report concerns an apparent crisis affecting the life chances of too many students and visited upon them by 'disruptive' students who need to be brought into line by teachers. However, much of these headline statements appear to come not from 3,000 inspections but rather largely from the YouGov surveys. In fact, as the Executive Summary clarifies, it is the surveys that 'show that pupils are potentially losing up to an hour of learning each day in English schools' (Ofsted 2014: 5), although it would be as fair to say that the surveys *claim* that pupils *might be* losing up to an hour.

Even the disruptive behaviours themselves (which include 'fidgeting' and 'talking unnecessarily') seem to have been defined by opinion polls rather than analysis and explicitly reinforce a set of traditional expectations of teachers and learners. Thus, when some teachers said that they ignored low-level disruption and just carried on, this is to be read only as a problem. And parents are co-opted merely to confirm this since 'parents consistently say that good discipline is the foundation stone of a good school'. Thus, when 'teachers blur the boundaries between friendliness and familiarity, for example by allowing the use of their first names' (Ofsted 2014: 6), there's bound to be trouble. At best these are stereotypes.

When a Primary School teacher is cited listing the paradigms of disruptive behaviour, she is apparently accessing an ahistorical motherlode of descriptive common sense: 'Children talking between themselves when they should be listening; fiddling with anything; writing when they should be listening; refusing to work with a talk partner' (Ofsted 2014: 7). These commonplaces of classroom management function as what Barthes deemed 'myth': their meanings constructed by collective (and long-term) consent in a process that transforms history into Nature. The simplicity (and sometimes simple-mindedness) of much of the debate around 'behaviour' and 'discipline' is a clue, for as Barthes suggested: 'Myth acts economically: it abolishes the complexity of human acts … it organises a world which is without contradictions because it is without depth' (Barthes 1972: 143). Barthes allocates to the 'mythologist' the job of mythifying the myth, proclaiming, 'What I claim is to live to the full the contradiction of my time, which may well make sarcasm the condition of truth' (Barthes 1972: 11).

Such sarcasm is hard to avoid when it comes to the report's account of 'disruption and the learner' and the grave news that a quarter of teachers 'thought it wasted at least five minutes per hour'. Some of the comments on students are hard to credit, for example the thought that teenagers might 'want to show off, are anti-establishment, or feel they have the right to be superior' or that 'pupils are not prepared to listen unless they are entertained' (Ofsted 2014: 7). These are merely opinions: Marshall McLuhan, for example, suggested that 'anyone who tries to make a distinction between education and entertainment doesn't know the first thing about either' (McLuhan 1967: 68). Parents also direct blame towards teachers although it's very difficult to see the validity of a methodology whereby one group of key witnesses are dependent for information on the group who are apparently causing the low-level disruption (students). The result is galling in the sense it shows clearly where the debate about teaching and learning currently is and it's not a bright place in either sense. It will need a context if it is to be understood.

Why teachers must not be classroom managers

In this chapter I am offering an explication of the long-term damage inflicted on notions of a rounded general education by this kind of thinking, whose 'sleight-of-hand' was to peaceably renegotiate the role of teacher from educator to 'classroom manager' with all that this now implies. In doing so I will also attempt to create what Foucault calls 'a history of the present' which is partly an updating development of Foucault's own 'history of the modern soul' in *Discipline and Punish* (Foucault 1995: 34) for these neo-liberal times. This history rejects notions of the master narrative of progress in favour of what Rose calls 'a number of contingent and altogether less refined and dignified practices' (Rose 1996: 129). As Kendall and Wickham explain: 'History should be used not to make ourselves comfortable but rather to disturb the taken for granted' (1999: 4). Much of this 'taken for granted' here concerns the basic sets of assumptions about why students are in schools or colleges, how they should behave there and what role teachers play in these important rituals. The genealogist works knowingly on 'a vast accumulation of source material' to problematize the discourses in this case surrounding behaviour and its management first by understanding these as 'contingent', that 'the emergence of that event was not necessary but was one possible result of a whole series of complex relations between other events' (Kendall and Wickham 1999: 5).

I cite, as part of that 'vast accumulation of source material', a personal and professional experience which, in Foucault's terms, is only now becoming a fact of history. I was teaching at a sixth-form college (running under school regulations) at the time and was required to attend an end-of-year staff conference at which we were invited to consider the novel proposition that we were all managers. This was 1994, ten years beyond Orwell's imagined nightmare of ultimate accountability, but also relatively early in the designation of head teachers and principals as 'managers'. As a group of largely advanced-level teachers we found the proposition that teachers might be 'classroom managers' as mere wordplay and probably a feeble attempt at cynical manipulation, and we said so in no uncertain terms (as teachers used to in the early 1990s). Now the notion of the teacher as a technician of 'classroom management' is a commonplace, although one which has in the minds of many teachers endangered the teaching function. What had seemed at the time a passing irritation has become in the fullness of time something much more sinister. With a combination of skill and sleight-of-hand the teacher had been reconstituted as a developer of human resources within the context of the industrial production market grade potential. And in the process the teacher had been set irreparably at odds with students, ironically reconstituted as 'learners' in the days after the failure of attempts to make 'customers' or 'clients' fit.

As Alex Kendall suggests: 'These sorts of ideas position teachers and learners in particular kinds of way' with teachers constituted as 'the "other" to the learner' (Kendall 2011: 227). This is a model not of responsiveness but rather of management and accountability in which 'the learner is construed as an 'anonymous, decontextualized, de-gendered being' whose '"responsibility" is to acquire "skills" which are atomised and ordered by hierarchical and linear arrangement' while the teacher's role is to 'determine a range of suitable teaching and learning techniques, manage the learning process, provide support to ensure the student meets the desired outcomes, and assess the outcomes of learning' (Kendall 2011: 228). Hence in Kendall's version the 'learner' is both disenfranchised and yet also 'cast as the central protagonist in their own drama of social and economic success': 'The student is offered a stake in what is known but not in, how it is known, who it is known by, whether it is worth knowing, or that there might be alternative ways of knowing' (Kendall 2011: 229).

Eve Tuck, a teacher educator from New York, sees in contemporary neo-liberal education policies defined by 'the relentless pursuit of accountability' the disenfranchisement/ downgrading of the teaching role such that his neo-liberal context is 'an unworkable framework for school reform and teacher education' (Tuck 2013: 324). Tuck shows how outwardly progressive policies like No Child Left Behind (Every Child Matters in the UK) 'directly contribute to school pushout' (exclusion) (Tuck 2013: 325). So too here, with 'having a calm and orderly environment for learning': inclusion quickly becomes exclusion in an almost Orwellian doublethink. Tuck controversially uses settler colonialism as the ultimate metaphor of dispossession with the undesirables (once the great unwashed) 'managed' out of their entitlements/birth right: 'settler colonialism is the context of the dispossession and erasure of poor youth and youth of color in urban public schools' (Tuck 2013: 326). Rather than 'the dispossession and erasure of Indigenous peoples, neo-liberalism as an extension of colonialism is concerned with the dispossession and erasure of the unworthy subject' (Tuck 2013: 341). This is Nick Peim's point too in his *Mythologies of Education*, though in a different key, and he sees this as part of education's 'deployment as population management', concerned with 'the distribution of identities within and for the social division of labour' (Peim 2013: 33).

These assumptions certainly pervade the Ofsted report above as does Peim's notion of education as a gift, though without Peim's 'problematic logic'. The point is that 'the obligations … of the gift of education are for life' and 'it is also clear that education is an offer that you cannot refuse' (Peim 2013: 33). And the punchline in this case is the same as it is for 'poor youth and youth of color' and their equivalents everywhere: 'In many cases, and for certain segments of the population it is also, at the same time, an offer you can't accept. Refusal is also no escape', identifying you 'as being in need of reorientation, salvation and realignment' (Peim 2013: 38). Tuck argues: 'Pedagogies such as Self-Regulated Learning can be seen to emerge from the same ideological context as self-service tills in supermarkets', including the implicit irony about who is being served and/or is regulating in each case (Tuck 2013: 331).

Figures in a landscape: some lessons in intellectual emancipation

The next historical fragment takes the form of a dramatized reconstruction of a professional encounter in Leicestershire in the 1990s between a teacher trainee and his placement mentor. Both, although they could hardly know it then, would later make significant contributions to a chapter in a book which sought to problematize ideas around 'classroom management' as a model of control because both have since written widely and perceptively about educational issues. However, back in the day the conversation was more narrowly about 'the kids' and the 'business' of being their teacher:

> Student teacher, Julian (now Professor of Media Education): 'I'll never control these kids, Nick.'
> Subject mentor and Head of English, Nick (now a widely published academic at a Russell Group university): 'Why on earth would you want to control them?'

But that is exactly what is expected of the contemporary teacher in every practical sense as both the epitome and entirety of their 'profession'. In exerting control over the behaviour of both their charges (dubbed 'learners' but more accurately 'subjects of learning') and their subject specialisms ('academic' largely as the dictionary defines; 'not of practical relevance; of only theoretical interest'), they are practising 'disciplines' of both sorts but most significantly demonstrating the self-discipline essential to their professional code of practice. Rancière argues in *The Ignorant Schoolmaster*: 'To emancipate an ignorant person, one must be, and one need only be, emancipated oneself' (Rancière 1991: 15), in other words that emancipating students require only a supply of emancipated teachers. In these neo-liberal times what appears to be the case is that what is similarly required for the intellectual enslavement and control of students is a reliable supply of teachers prepared to be themselves controlled. Hence Thomas writes: 'The surveillance of students, and now the surveillance of teachers (and ultimately of all citizens of a corporate state), is not covert, but in plain view in the form of tests, that allow that surveillance to be disembodied from those students and teachers – and thus appearing to be impersonal – and examined as if objective and a reflection of merit' (Thomas 2013: 215).

Tuck understands this process as 'a narrowing of the activities of schooling, to what can be measurable' which 'renders teaching and learning as technological tasks', 'components of an ideologically driven agenda that is fundamentally redefining what it means to be a teacher in the U.S.' (Tuck 2013: 110). This is entirely Foucault's model of subjection and to a lesser degree Rancière's notion of stultification. For the poet William Blake energy was 'eternal delight' but Blake was a creator. The 'discipline' involved in contemporary schooling is explicitly conservative, intent on channelling potentially disruptive energy into 'shoulder to the wheel' conformity: hence Foucault's explanation that 'discipline increases the forces of the body (in economic terms of utility) and diminishes these same forces (in political terms of obedience)' (Foucault 1995: 149). Foucault writes about the ways in which discipline fosters both docility and productivity: the best of both worlds for those who would like us to see education as the key to economic prosperity. Nick Peim (he who was earlier questioning the desire to control and now a significant voice from the academy) sees this as a clever deceit with its underlying instrumental rationality. In arguing that education is the master-myth of our time, operating as 'a Heideggerian onto-theological principle' (something we must believe in rather than critically apprehend), Nick Peim identifies among 'a series of specific myths in a turbulent system of differences, the myth of economic prosperity' (Peim 2013: 32). Here 'policy buys into the mythology that equates investment in education with future prosperity and with the implicit project of social justice', even though education in modernity 'is fatally neo-liberal, structurally organized to maintain growing economic inequalities' (Peim 2013: 39).

The uses of literacy (and illiteracy) in the age of anxiety

This is not a secret history but it may, in some ways, be a shameful one. When Richard Hoggart wrote his ground-breaking book *The Uses of Literacy: Aspects of Working-Class Life* in 1957, he was drawing on his own experience as a 'clever' working-class kid growing up in Hunslet, a district of Leeds (one of those clever poor kids who are now being outstripped in school by 'thick' rich kids in popular scare stories which are really diversions). In the second part of chapter ten, 'Unbent Strings: A Note on the Uprooted and the Anxious', he considers the very shock troops of the meritocracy, the scholarship boys (those who got to better schools by passing academic tests). To Hoggart, even those whose place in the managed scheme is 'advanced' are compromised by an education which fails to convince those emotionally uprooted from their class in a world where in one sense, no one is ever 'declassed'.

These boys still exist and in greater numbers in our new inclusive model of education and are joined by many (probably many more) girls and yet the outcomes are often the same; they become 'uncertain, dissatisfied, and gnawed by self-doubt' (Hoggart 1957: 293). Such issues are precisely those that a centralized predetermined National Curriculum is unwilling and/or unable to address. What increasingly needs to be 'managed' are the discrepancies between this theory and the practical demands of these post-/super-/hyper-modern times. Rather than ask who our 'learners' are, we list what they need to know and even more importantly plot how they are meant to develop so their progress can be monitored and managed. In Peim's terms: 'Education tells us both what are and, more disturbingly, what we should be' (Peim 2013: 33) and most significantly that 'self-improvement requires a structuring and context for its effective operation' (Peim 2013: 37).

Thus, there is an unwillingness or inability to deal even with the present at a time when the Italian philosopher Franco Berardi is suggesting that young people have lost any kind of feasible idea of the future. He claims further: 'Corporate capitalism and neoliberal ideology have produced lasting damage in the material structures of the world and in the social, cultural, and nervous systems of mankind' (Berardi 2011: 8). And all this as a result of the failure of education to provide fundamental things like an active culture, a vibrant public sphere and forms of collective imagination (Berardi 2011: 9). Instead we find fear, including fear of failure, and those who Hoggart identified as 'gnawed by self-doubt' reconstituted as the mainstream. Writing of our 'hyper-modern times' the French philosopher Lipovetsky declares that 'a sense of insecurity has invaded all of our minds' (Lipovetsky 2005: 13). Berardi is concerned at the way in which, for example, student debt operates as a kind of blackmail, forcing people into 'any kind of precarious job' in this time of 'finance capitalism and precarious salaries' (Berardi 2015).

Lipovetsky stresses the importance of understanding the hypermodern individual whom Berardi typifies as 'a smiling, lonely monad who walks in the urban space in tender continuous interaction with the photos, the tweets, the games that emanate from a personal screen' (Berardi 2015). Lipovetsky offers a similar version which stresses the contradictory character of our potential learners: 'Hypermodern individuals are both better informed and even more deconstructed, more adult and more unstable, less ideological and more in thrall to changing fashions, more open and easier to influence, more critical and more superficial, more sceptical and less profound' (Lipovetsky 2005: 5). And teachers must resolve all of this armed only with a curriculum that seeks to retreat to modified versions of a half-imagined past.

Hoggart's dismay is palpable and, over sixty years later, we can only share his concern for the contemporary 'learner' who 'tends to over-stress the importance of examinations, of the piling-up of knowledge and of received opinion' and 'discovers a technique of apparent learning, of the acquiring of facts rather than of the handling and use of facts' (Hoggart 1957: 297). In simple terms, for Hoggart: 'He has been trained like a circus-horse'. This is discipline, indeed, and long known, as Hoggart himself looks back to philosopher and sociologist Herbert Spencer fifty years before him. Spencer brands the 'established systems of education' as 'fundamentally vicious in their manner' and considers that they 'encourage submissive receptivity instead of independent activity' (Hoggart 1957: 298).

Michael Gove achieved notoriety as Education Secretary by, among other things, suggesting that he would never let evidence get in the way of a policy he knew to be the right one. He largely, though, escaped ridicule for his campaign for a knowledge-based curriculum, although its catchy slogan 'Facts, facts, facts' was taken directly from the mouth of that Dickensian grotesque Thomas Gradgrind (the grade-grinder), a satirical embodiment and indictment of the kind of education that Gove was striving to resuscitate. This 'man of realities' (Gradgrind not Gove) is named in a chapter entitled 'Murdering the Innocents' (in case you miss the mode of address: irony is a dangerous weapon), the chapter that also introduces the trainee teacher M'Choakumchild (not shy of discipline this one) whose many 'knowledges' Dickens perceptively dismisses with the following: 'Ah, rather overdone, M'Choakumchild. If he had only learned a little less, how infinitely better he might have taught much more' (Dickens). This was 1854 and has resonance still as a critique of the overburdening of teachers with 'stuff' rather than 'scope'.

Creating subject identities and identities for subjects

Dickens is capturing something of the essence of the Victorian project of Elementary schooling, unashamedly an initiative which sought to shape and control: to domesticate not liberate. Peim writes of 'a well-ordered, morally-managed future' in which the rougher sorts 'could be remade as more or less self-regulating, more or less good and loyal citizens' (Peim 2013: 34). This confirms Kendall and Wickham's Foucaultian reading of the emergence of the classroom not 'as an attempt to foster the liberal, free, rational individual or as a result of the working class's efforts to educate and politicize itself' but rather 'concerned with the management of lives, not the meanings they drew on or left aside' (Kendall and Wickham 1999: 123). The discomfort comes not from the limited character of these earliest moves in the direction of mass education but rather from the galling contemporaneity of these accounts of historical practice; this is, indeed, a history of the present. Take Kendall and Wickham: 'This type of schooling was profoundly bureaucratic and disciplinary rather than democratic or progressive revolutionary' (Kendall and Wickham 1999), or Peim: 'They would be basically numerate and literate, manually skilled, mostly well-fed and imbued with national values' (Peim 2013: 34).

Peim goes on to flesh out the ways in which this became normalized. These include 'the definition of norms of progress and curriculum content, the deployment of pastoral discipline within the enclosed social space of the classroom, the ethic of self-managed motivation, the hortatory style of the assembly, the organization of the playground as the meeting point for the culture of the child with the culture of the school' (Peim 2013: 34). Here is the paraphernalia of classroom management where those who are performance-managed manage performance. Peim complains that 'the child's very being is being charted on the grid of what already has been decided counts as developmentally significant' (Peim 2013: 35) to which we must add; as the teacher's very being is. For it is true in our contemporary context that 'maturity here is not achieved in the form of independence from the grid, the norms and the agents of judgment' but rather 'through bringing one's identity in line with the judgments made and orienting one's trajectory and one's aspirations accordingly' (Peim 2013: 35).

For Peim the idea of the teacher 'cultural worker in close social proximity to her charges, was developed as the key instrument of "governmentality"' since 'the kindly disciplinarian dispenses education as the necessary correction of your wayward tendencies' (Peim 2013: 34). Again, the focus is not on what you need to know because 'curriculum content hardly matters' but 'what you need to do and to be. You will be educated above all in the norms of conduct befitting your social destiny' (Peim 2013: 34).

In *Discipline and Punish*, Foucault (1995) explores the history of discipline and the disciplines, charting the change from the use of torture to more 'gentle punishments which attempted to control populations by creating oppositions within them. These oppositions were manufactured in places like schools, hospitals and prisons, wherein reside those Foucault dubbed 'the judges of normality':

The judges of normality are present everywhere. We are in the society of the teacher-judge, the doctor-judge, the educator-judge, the social worker-judge; it is on them that the universal reign of the normative is based; and each individual, wherever he may find himself, subjects to it his body, his gestures, his behavior, his aptitudes, his achievements. (Foucault 1995: 304)

This is not about justice and fairness (or even injustice and unfairness) but about the representation and material enactment of social power. This is Foucault's central interest, and ours; how modern society creates subject identities by management and discipline in the context of ideas about normality inculcated in institutions like the school and regulated by 'qualified' professionals, and the judgement of professionals. Foucault's project is to write 'a correlative history of the modern soul and of a new power to judge; a genealogy of the present scientifico-legal complex from which the power to punish derives its bases, justifications and rules' (Foucault 1995: 23).

That portion of the 'scientifico-legal complex' deemed 'education' is intensely involved in what Foucault calls a 'specific mode of subjection', a particular version of the process by which we are 'produced' as subjects. Here we get to the real issue of teacher accountability and the increasing focus on classroom management since the focus is no longer on education but rather on 'subjection', no longer on exploration but rather on 'treatment'. Here discipline and punishment systems are productive of particular kinds of knowledge and essentially political, a way of enacting power.

For Foucault, discipline and disciplines are a means of producing 'docile bodies', whether that compliance is strategic or not. This produces the economic ideal more productive 'bodies' which are also easier to control on a mass scale: 'If economic exploitation separates the force and the product of labour, let us say that disciplinary coercion establishes in the body the constricting link between an increased aptitude and an increased domination' (Foucault 1995: 138). Discipline is political: 'a political anatomy of detail', making individuals both as objects and as instruments of its exercise, a 'modest, suspicious power' (Foucault 1995: 170). It works through hierarchical observation ('an architecture that is not built to be seen, but to see others'), by normalizing judgement: 'Crimes of non-observance are created. One is made guilty for omission, the things you didn't do' and the examination (for Foucault both school test and hospital consultation) which 'combines the techniques of an observing hierarchy and those of a normalizing judgment' (Foucault 1995: 184). Discipline is in this way a form of power which works through sight, not physical force.

We are living at a moment where 'the examination' as both a generality and a specific experience has never been so important. Foucault helps us to understand why it has such a key role in the 'management' of populations aside from just being a way for professionals to assert their authority. Fundamentally, the exam turns people into analysable objects and forces them within a comparative system, transforming 'the economy of visibility into the exercise of power' (Foucault 1995: 187). Foucault writes of the documentary techniques, which make each individual a case. As we are written up in the record, so we are made visible and disempowered by being managed: incorporated rather than accommodated. In this way, as Peim points out 'education promotes a maniacally norm-related model of knowledge, identity and development' (Peim 2013: 39). And those who resist this management by classification will be pursued as 'abnormals', requiring 'special' education or simply correction.

Back to the future: setting things in context

We must not though let talk of 'remorseless logic' allow us to see these events as inevitable rather than contextualized and contingent. Casting back for models as the traditionalists are wont to do, I can easily unearth a couple of examples of another view, progressive and resistant. The first is the cult 1960s TV series *The Prisoner* which explicitly explored much of the ground that Foucault would very soon afterwards explore with eloquent clarity. *The Prisoner* is an object lesson in the representation of 'a multiplicity of often minor processes, of different origin and scattered location, which overlap, repeat, or imitate one another, support one another, distinguish themselves from one another according to their domain of application, converge and gradually produce the blueprint of a general method' (Foucault 1995: 138). What Number Six ('naming is incriminating') experiences in The Village, his place of gentle punishments, is continual frustrating evidence that 'discipline is a political anatomy of detail'. And his response is the one we might require from fellow teachers and students all, 'I will not be pushed, filed, stamped, indexed, briefed, debriefed, or numbered! My life is my own!' (cue *maniacal laughter*). The other source is equally adamant and resistant, although its source is not well known as the voice of progressive social policy. Lest we think that the modern trend of teachers 'owning' their results and school league tables is a given, it is worth checking the archive and specifically a speech that the Duke of Edinburgh gave to the Association of Technical Institutions in 1964 which reflected: 'It seems to be fashionable to choose the success rate in examinations as a criterion for judging the performance of schools' (quoted in Lowe 2007: 40). Remorseless logic? Actually no, since he went on to say: 'This might be convenient but makes a mockery of education in its widest sense.'

Education 'in its widest sense', as we have seen, is not exactly the priority in our neo-liberal times but that doesn't excuse us as teachers from ignoring or even side-stepping our ethical responsibilities. We must resist the common sense of classroom management just as we resist performance management because they are essentially the same thing. In other words, we need to renegotiate the fundamental relationship between teachers and students in the interest of equality and social justice. In his essay 'The Distribution of the Sensible' Jacques Rancière points out: 'Politics revolves around what is seen and what can be said about it, around who has the ability to see and the talent to speak' (Rancière 2006: 8). His *Five Lessons in Intellectual Emancipation* are a set of radical practices designed to expect this ability and talent from all participants in education. Rancière subjects teaching basics to a remorseless critique, for example, the proposition that 'to teach was to transmit learning and form minds simultaneously, by leading those minds, according to an ordered progression, from the most simple to the most complex' (Rancière 1991: 3). This, he feels, like all of education, was predicated on what he called 'the myth of pedagogy, the parable of a world divided into knowing minds and ignorant ones, ripe minds and immature ones, the capable and the incapable, the intelligent and the stupid' (Rancière 1991: 6).

For Rancière this belief in an inferior intelligence and a superior one creates limitation, dependency ('To explain something to someone is first of all to show him he cannot understand it by himself' (Rancière 1991: 6)) and effectively puts paid to notions of equality, which are shuffled into a redemptive future. Rancière presents a simple premise, which turns out in the current dispensation to be the most exacting and for some teachers the least feasible: 'To emancipate an ignorant person, one must be, and one need only be, emancipated oneself' (Rancière 1991: 15). His model of 'universal teaching' offers the very antithesis of the current norm-related model of knowledge, identity and development:

> This is the way that the ignorant master can instruct the learned one as well as the ignorant one: by verifying that he is always searching. Whoever looks always finds. He doesn't necessarily find what he was looking for, and even less what he was supposed to find. But he finds something new to relate to the thing that he already knows. (Rancière 1991: 33)

Postscript: towards a community of equals

It is an approach based on dignity and trust, a 'Community of Equals', 'society of the emancipated that would … repudiate the division between those who know and those who don't, between those who possess or don't possess the property of intelligence' (Rancière 1991: 71). Rancière speaks of 'the particular application of the power common to all reasonable beings, the one that each person feels when he withdraws into that privacy of consciousness where lying makes no sense' (Rancière 1991). In an era of G scores, prescriptive subject content and high-risk exams, Rancière's invective seems strangely prescient: 'There are no madmen except those who insist on inequality and domination, those who want to be right' (Rancière 1991: 72). Rather than predicate a system on classification and rank, Rancière proposes an alternative based instead on equality, which may offer a better place to begin the recovery:

> It is true that we don't know that men are equal. We are saying that they might be. This is our opinion, and we are trying, along with those who think as we do, to verify it. But we know that this might, is the very thing, that makes a society of humans possible. (Rancière 1991: 73)

Do you think we could manage that?

Activities

1   List and probe the different ways in which 'manager' and 'management' are used in your institution and/or in schools, colleges and universities more broadly. Who or what is being managed here?

2   Explore the ways in which subject disciplines promote compliance and conformity.

3   What do you think Foucault means when he provocatively suggests that discipline is 'political'?

References

Barthes, R. (1972), *Mythologies*, London: Jonathon Cape.

Berardi, F. (2011), *After the Future*, Chico, CA: AK Press.

Berardi, F. (2015), *Heroes: Mass Murder and Suicide*, London: Verso. E-book.

Duke of Edinburgh (1964), 'Presidential Address to the Association of Technical Institutions', *Times Educational Supplement*, 21 February 1964.

Foucault, M. (1995), *Discipline and Punish*, London: Vintage.

Hoggart, R. (1957), *The Uses of Literacy*, London: Chatto & Windus.

Kendall, A. (2011), 'Pedagogy After the Media: Towards a "Pedagogy of the Inexpert"', in P. Bennett, A. Kendall and J. McDougall (eds), *After the Media: Culture and Identity in the 21st Century*, London: Routledge.

Kendall, G., and Wickham, G. (1999), *Using Foucault's Methods*, London: Sage.

Lipovetsky, G. (2005), *Hypermodern Times*, Cambridge: Polity.

Lowe, R. (2007), *The Death of Progressive Education: How Teachers Lost Control of the Classroom*, Abingdon: Routledge.

McLuhan, M. (1967), 'The New Education', *The Basilian Teacher*, 11 (2): 66–73.

Ofsted (2014), *Below the Radar: Low-Level Disruption in the Country's Classrooms*. Available online: http://www.ofsted.gov.uk/resources/below-radar-low-level-disruption-country%E2%80%99s-classrooms (accessed 23 April 2018).

Peim, N. (2013), 'Education as Mythology', in P. Bennett and J. McDougall (eds), *Barthes' Mythologies Today: Readings of Contemporary Culture*, Abingdon: Routledge.

Rancière, J. (1991), *The Ignorant Schoolmaster: Five Lessons in Intellectual Emancipation*, Stanford: Stanford University Press.

Rancière, J. (2006), *The Politics of Aesthetics*, London: Continuum.

Rose, N. (1996), 'Identity, Genealogy, History', in S. Hall (ed.), *Questions of Cultural Identity*, London: Sage.

Thomas, P.L. (2013), 'Corporate Education Reform and the Rise of State Schools', *Journal for Critical Education Policy Studies*, 11 (2): 203–238.

Tuck, E. (2013), 'Neoliberalism as Nihilism? A Commentary on Educational Accountability, Teacher Education, and School Reform', *Journal for Critical Education Policy Studies*, 11 (2): 324–347.

3 Reflections on the Language of Disruption, Learning and Conflict

MERV LEBOR

Setting out the territory

In this chapter, I explore the problematics of the language we use when discussing negative situations in classrooms and how this constructs our understanding of 'disruption'. I begin by commenting on difficulties of defining learning and various ways in which it can be disrupted. I discuss the complex nature of violent classroom events, show differences between school and college contexts and explore the implications of different pedagogic relationships. I analyse how writers have used the language of conflict to describe disruptive behaviour within educational contexts. There is finally a section discussing some strategies for defusing disruptions and conflicts in the classroom.

I have been reflecting publicly on the issues of what hinders 'learning' from taking place in classrooms for many years (e.g. Lebor 2000, 2014, 2017), but dealing with the problems involved for far longer. However, this discussion assumes that there is an agreed view of what 'learning' is, so we can determine whether it is being disrupted. Learning is a highly contested notion often ideologically constructed in terms of *inter alia* Behaviourist, Cognitivist, Constructivist and Humanist, deep, surface, rote or acculturated processes. For the purposes of this essay, I use the *Oxford English Dictionary* definition: 'The acquisition of knowledge or skills through study, experience, or being taught.' There are also a variety of levels of intensity by which learning, however defined, can be perceived as being disrupted. The word perceived is crucial because what is considered as disruptive by certain teachers, managers, observers or Ofsted might be normative, productive learning by others (Ofsted 2014; Dfe 2012).

At its most extreme, disruption can involve violence against teachers. This is a relatively rare phenomenon, particularly in the post-school sector; however, it can present difficulties within Pupil Referral Units (PRUs) or special facilities for supporting potentially 'aggressive' learners who cannot cope with the conventional norms of classroom interactions. The problem is that we are seeing more so-called vulnerable students enter our colleges (Wolf 2011). Most teacher education, however, is concerned with the norms of how, where and when learning can best take place (Gravells and Simpson 2014; Petty 2014; Avis et al. 2015); my personal interest is in those points where learning is resisted.

Learning can be disrupted in numerous ways. After attacks on teachers, the next level of intensity is violence between students, screaming, refusal to carry out tasks, talking in class, using mobile phones, putting on make-up, coming late or, arguably, the ultimate vote of no confidence in the teaching, not turning up for lessons (Parry and Taubman 2013). Context is everything. Each of the above scenarios could be perfectly legitimate learning experiences. The violence between students could be martial arts. The screaming could be on the football field. Refusal to carry out tasks might be assertiveness training. Using a mobile could be research or part of a Kahoot-style quiz (an online games platform for learning purposes). Talking in class could be paired work, discussion or a team project. Lateness might represent genuine problems; the student could be the caring lynch-pin in the survival of his/her family. Putting on make-up could be on a beauty course. Not attending could be due to disability, distance learning or even students completing course work. Some students work better in an independent digital environment and achieve higher marks when working from home. Nevertheless, the above scenarios need scrutiny and subsequently, I will offer strategies for dealing with these potentially fraught situations.

However, the debate in this essay is whether it is helpful to use the language of violence as a metaphor for describing classroom disruptions, but also explore strategies to prepare teachers for dealing with these challenging circumstances. To some extent, violent language is unavoidable because, at its most extreme, when students attack each other physically, it is unrealistic to discuss classroom events and not report on violent realities. For example, I interviewed four teachers who reported large-scale violence at their separate secondary schools. Shockingly, in one case their school's students were involved in pitched battles with another school every evening for three months. In two other schools, fights were large-scale internal affairs, involving more than forty students. Teachers and police tried to break up these conflicts, but the dynamic of what witnesses termed as 'race wars' was not easily stemmed. Few of these stories made the newspapers, but students' lives and learning were deeply disrupted (e.g. Yorkshire Evening Post 2014). Many students were scared to go to school.

It should be said that there are commercial, social and psychological sensitivities highlighting problems in these contexts. If institutions are associated with violence, students will be disinclined to enrol. The implications are that there are deep ethical implications to any investigation into this area (BERA 2018). It is arguably better to compromise the validity of research than to expose the realities of what is happening in specific contexts through identifying institutions or individuals. However, the more specificity is given to incidents, the more the person, area or incident can be identified. Reporting on violence in classrooms is literally fraught with dangers.

My point is that extreme events do happen in both school and post-school contexts which are difficult to discuss without using imagery of violence where this is actually happening. Overall these cases are aberrations. Most post-school students are compliant (Ofsted 2014); society is well-schooled, rather than de-schooled (Illich 1971). However, there is often low-level disruption to learning and a growing sense that trainee tutors are reporting on disruptive classes but are being ignored (Lebor 2017: 169–186).

The complex nature of violent events

Before the 1990s one might argue that the violence was from teachers towards students. Corporal punishment was the norm. Students were hit with hard objects, including sticks, canes and board rubbers. By 1998 violence against students was banned in state and private schools (BBC 1998). After this date punishments had to be non-physical, operating within the affective domain. Student violence, however, continued. At its worst it could be the murderous attack on Anne Maguire in Leeds (Guardian 2017), but it is significant that this event attracted national news coverage for its rarity and outrageous injustice. Nevertheless, there are still violent incidents described between students in schools and colleges (ATL 2016). In my own experience, violence is a deeply disturbing, complex social event. I personally have a deep aversion or even chill when witnessing these incidents but am constantly drawn back possibly to confront what I fear most.

A 19-year-old female student, 'Jan', from an impoverished background in a Foundation learning unit hit another female student on the head with an iron bar in a corridor during lunch break. Jan was said to be 'disturbed'. One could have asked her therapeutic questions about her childhood and self-esteem issues (Ecclestone 2009). There could be motivational analysis. Was Jan looking for attention? Did she need containment or have boundary issues? Was the abuse in her background now playing out in social situations? Or we could ask managerial questions, such as does human behaviour always need policing? Should all teachers be taught counselling? But then which version? Would therapy have saved Jan's brain-damaged victim?

A 21-year-old Access student from an affluent background kicked cars and threatened teachers (Lebor 2017). The teacher attempted a mixture of counselling models in order to integrate this student into getting through his assessment. A GCSE Maths student, Angela, threatened to 'kick teachers' if they didn't do what she said. Her wealthy father blamed teachers, previously at school and now at college for 'not engaging' his daughter sufficiently. There were financial implications to the college if they expelled her. Management decided that the current Maths teacher needed support in the classroom to work with Angela independently.

The points are that violent behaviour is the provenance of wealth as well as deprivation. There are financial implications to excluding students from college. It could be argued that if students threaten violence, the 'punishment' must be expulsion because it's an issue of safeguarding staff and students. The problem is that if expelled from class, will the student merely wander the corridors, causing more disruption? If expelled from college, are we merely channelling these students towards criminality? How do we keep difficult students in education rather than excluding them?

The other problem is that if tutors are not aware of psychological approaches to interpersonal relationships, then their engagement with students will lack nuance or emotional intelligence (Goleman 1999). On the other hand, if teachers take a counselling approach to these difficult students, then the question becomes whether they are thoroughly trained in each stage of the model they follow and where they might breach the line between teaching and counselling.

A teacher walks into class and all desks are immediately kicked over. A female student physically attacks a smaller male because he doesn't share her taste in music. Violence is sometimes unpredictable. In my view trainee teachers need to explore (and experienced practitioners share) case study after case study. The reason is so that even if these events never happen during their career, teacher education should be preparing trainees not merely for their current placement, but for potentially demanding circumstances throughout the sector. Not preparing trainees for this is, in my view, a dereliction of duty (Lebor 2017).

Differences between school and college

The problem is that most advice on classroom management is based in the school rather than post-school sector (Ellis and Tod 2014). There are many differences. To summarize:

- School teachers are always older than their pupils. This has many implications. For example, the advice in schools is often to speak to the parents (Bennet 2015); in college the disruptive students could be parents.
- Further Education (FE) teachers can be younger than their students. Students can be disruptive because they don't respect teachers who are less experienced, but in a position of authority over them.
- Schools are usually on one site; there are bells, uniforms, assemblies, usually 1,000 to 2,000 students at the very most.
- Colleges could have 20,000 students in different towns.
- A college principal rarely addresses all students at once, unless it is, for example, a small countryside institution.
- Colleges are focused mainly on vocational courses with academic strands; schools are mostly academic with vocational strands.
- Unless home-schooled or certain other (sometimes hidden) minorities, everyone goes through the school system experience; not everyone goes to college.

The implications of these infrastructural differences are numerous. Both systems can be fraught with conflicts, rivalries and human difficulties. However,

- It is much harder to impose a whole institution approach on a college than in a school because there can be a large span of ages, many socio-economic backgrounds.
- The atmosphere and culture in an engineering department is very different to beauty, flower-arranging or Advanced Level literature in college.
- The vocational nature of college means that beliefs, behaviours and cultures tend to be more diverse.
- Pupils spend five years at secondary school; college students could be there for two years, a month, a week or a day.
- At school, because of the timescale and location, students and teachers are more well-known to each other.
- There can be personalities among teachers notorious for their imposition of authority or students for their misdemeanours. Such people in college would usually be known only to a select few.
- In schools the control mechanisms tend to be greater.
- There are few punishments available in colleges.

Yet colleges have now tightened security on doors, name tabs and electronic means of entering college buildings and classrooms.

In schools and colleges teachers use schemes of work, lesson plans and resources to support learning. The assumption is that if these structures are in place, then learning will happen (Beere 2012). The problem is that just because teachers teach does not mean learners learn.

Class management taught by single lecture

To reiterate, I believe behaviour management should be taught as a compulsory part of teachers' training courses. Teacher education departments, however, often teach behaviour management to post-school teacher trainees as a one-off lecture. I attended two such lectures. The first male lecturer exuded macho violence. He was forceful and acted out gestures, attitudes and strategies for imposing authority on potentially recalcitrant students. The problems were:

- The listeners cannot inhabit his personality in their classrooms.
- They may not share the same dominance patterns, personal attitudes or humour.
- Sometimes the more authoritarian the teacher, the more students can refuse to co-operate.
- Each teacher and class is existentially different. One can't legislate; what works in one class will not necessarily work elsewhere.

Wallace (2017) rightly suggests logging when and with whom specific strategies worked or did not. However, the same tactic might not work with the same group twice.

The second lecturer used Bill Rogers's school-based book (2015) as a model for lecturers working in FE and Higher Education (HE). One major difference between school and post-school is the issue of proxemics. How close do we get to students? This female lecturer approached women on the front row, to demonstrate how they might intimidate students to stop them speaking, as also suggested by Petty (2014: 99). The problem is:

- In an adult environment this becomes overtly an issue of space invasion.
- Women teachers coming close to male students or male teachers coming close to female students can be perceived as an intrusion.

This is probably true in schools, but physical proximity in the adult world is more loaded, having implications of physical or sexual aggression. However, this dimension is never discussed in most teacher education textbooks (Gravells and Simpson 2014; Petty 2014).

Constructing behaviour management

The language we use about teaching constructs our attitudes towards being tutors in classrooms. Even the word 'disruption' implies there is a flow that is being stopped in some way, but, sometimes intrusions into the rhythm of a session can develop the meaning of the learning involved. However, disruptions can be irritating for other learners in the classroom. Even the term 'behaviour management' implies students cannot be self-directed or independent but must be controlled. The word 'behaviour' potentially places the concept within the sphere of Behaviourism (Lebor 2017: 193). The words construct the pedagogic relationship. In this section I explore some language I and others have used about behaviour management and its implications for how teachers are existentially present in classrooms.

A key work on behaviour management *Getting the Buggers to Behave* (Cowley 2014) dispenses good advice, based on classroom experience, albeit predominantly in the school sector. The title, however, is problematic, expressing humorous frustration and exasperation, but possibly anger and contempt for students. The model of student/teacher relationship it constructs is one of teacher-power threatened, but ultimately reasserting its authority. The use of the word 'bugger' by Wallace (2007), with its homophobic implications and construction of negative behaviour as purely the provenance of male students, possibly shows a highly gendered understanding of the sector.

Lebor's article 'Class Wars' (2013) described violent incidents, but ironically plays on the Marxist idea of class conflict, implying the clash between middle-class expectations of education being foisted on 'working-class' students (Hyland 2006). The use of violent language objectifies or even distances classroom problems through humour as a defence against chilling acts of physical violence. The problem with this language is that it constructs the relationship between teacher and student as one of conflict. There are many alternative ways of envisioning these events and relationships.

Models of being a teacher

The classic language of behaviour management is associated with Kounin whose famous concepts of 'withitness', momentum, pace, focus, ripple and satiety, constructs teachers as dynamic, all-seeing gods who can control time, space and people within the confines of their classrooms (1997). This potentially offers engaging sessions where differentiated students are constantly involved in learning activities. This is obviously ideal, but:

- It assumes activities are meaningful and students are not merely being kept busy.
- It is not particularly contemplative.
- It doesn't say what happens if students do not comply.
- It assumes all teachers have dynamic personalities.

Other models of being a teacher also exist (Table 3.1). The authoritarian model constructs teachers as Dickensian instructors conveying information to students, tightly controlling all behaviour. The power is with the teacher. Military-trained tutors seem to develop voices that will not be disobeyed. The problem is whether students are offered enough space to evolve independent personalities in this environment. At the other extreme there is the Summerhill experiment (Hemmings 1972); however, does complete freedom help students become part of our contemporary, commercial-industrial complex?

Another model is teacher as revolutionary, encouraging disaffected students to rebel because their disruptive behaviour could be understood as dissatisfaction with capitalism. At its most productive, this could work as transformative education that is now normative in much educational thinking (Freire 1972). Alternatively, teachers could be constructed as counsellors. The problem is that each model of therapy has its own strictures. If psycho-dynamic, have all teachers gone through transference? If Cognitive Behavioural Therapy or Solution Focus, do teachers know all the stages that each student must go through before being 'cured' or achieve self-esteem (Hyland 2006)? Are teachers supposed to get students to express or suppress their feelings? Context is again crucial.

Many theorists construct teachers as managing learning (Wong 2009). The positives are:

- This prepares students for the workplace.
- It implies fewer authoritarian classrooms.
- It creates adult environments where self-directed learning prevails (Knowles 1975).

The critique of this model centres on the overwhelming influence of managerialism, performativity and capitalism permeating education (Ball 2003). The defence of using

Table 3.1 Models of teaching

Style	Benefits	Possible drawbacks
Authoritarian teacher	Total control, emphasis on teaching rather than learning. Teacher is all-commanding/dominant figure. Culture of obedience.	How do we know students are actually learning? What space is there for students to express themselves? Will students rebel or reject authority figures.
Students' freedom of choice on how to learn	Self-directed learning/potentially very powerful as students motivated to learn rather than being forced.	Issue of containment/teacher direction and boundaries. Will students socialise instead of studying? Will the students learn the required syllabus and pass exams?
'Revolutionary' teaching	Teacher as catalyst for transformation of character, social class and economic status of students.	This might be threatening for status quo; could potentially encourage disruption of other tutors' lessons. Could lead to chaotic situations or reversal of power on teachers.
Teacher as counsellor	Supportive attitude, seeing problems of students as needing psychological and emotional solutions rather than punishment.	Assumes one-to-one attention possible. Which model of therapy? Many models of therapy are contradictory. Are teachers sufficiently qualified to apply one method systematically? Bad behaviour rewarded with more intensive attention.
Teacher as facilitator	Managing classrooms, modelling work-based business version of training. Preparing students for the world of work. Humanising/adult attitude to students.	This assumes that students will co-operate and have adult attitudes. It is also the managerialism of capitalism now embedded into much education culture.

the facilitator as a helpful image is that this reflects the dominant discourse of neo-liberal society and student acculturation into our contemporary world (Avis et al. 2015).

Strategies

Teachers face complex relationships with difficult individuals and yet have enormous demands placed on them, including embedding Equality and Diversity; group profiling; core curricula of Maths, literacy and ICT; British values; safeguarding; professional standards; Prevent; lesson plans; schemes of work; awareness of quality-based observations; and Ofsted requirements, yet still be able to have a relationship with individual students, conveying an inclusive curriculum. But within the post-school sector, if students don't comply are there punishments available? Is punishment even the right approach? If permanent exclusion is the most extreme action an institution can take, what support are we setting up for those students who find themselves disempowered, excluded or, for a multitude of reasons, find it difficult to fit in?

The age of abusive, corporal punishment is finished. So, what responses are available in the supposed more adult environment of a college? Violence within institutions, assault, sexual harassment, pornography or bullying are matters to be reported to safeguarding officers within college and may turn out to be police concerns. This dimension is, unfortunately, the context we inhabit. Before exclusion from college with all its social, financial and emotional consequences, there can be the option of asking students to leave the room. The difficulty is that the student then roams free on corridors. Punishments, if necessary, must be administered within a highly monitored framework or they could prove counter-productive, un-educational and destroy relationships.

The issuing of warnings, even contacting parents (subject to the age of the student and permission to contact parents), sending students to speak to managers, but preferably counsellors, could be the next option. Other strategies might involve ignoring disruptive students, focusing on those students who are engaged, but then this might precipitate more 'bad behaviour' from the individuals who are not conforming. Again, not smiling or smiling at the 'disruptive' student might be equally devastating. Having extensive after-class discussions with the student about why they acted disruptively, what they hope to get from the course and then how best this could be achieved is part of much normative teaching. The ultimate punishment could be the student failing, but this could also be understood as a failure of the teacher.

Better enrolment processes could help to avoid disruptive behaviour at a later stage, ensuring that initially students are on courses for which they have at least an affinity if not a career aspiration (Wallace 2013). Much disruption comes from the fact that college students are often doing subjects for which they have neither aptitude nor interest. Career advice, understandings of what individuals want must be central to initial interviews and student selection. Secondly, at enrolment the clear parameters of what is expected must be set out, understood and contracted for each individual student.

On entry into the classroom a meet-and-greet policy at the door can create a sense of connection. This is not always possible if students are already in their seats and some cultures do not encourage proximity or even handshakes inter or intra gender. Some students just do not like teachers intruding into their body space. Nevertheless, the beginnings of a relationship between teacher and student can be established at the classroom door. It is part of the process of 'getting to know your students' (Petty 2014: 484–486).

The next stage of 'getting to know students' is via using name tabs on the desk. Each student should be given a sheet of paper to fold on which they write the name by which they wish to be called. The name tabs face outwards towards the class/front, so that the tutor can easily call each student by their first name. This is vital so that the teacher can address and question everyone by name particularly if they are acting in a disruptive way. Vaguely shouting 'you!' at someone who is not engaged in the lesson is ineffective, insulting, exposes the lack of relationship between tutor and student, but also ultimately diminishes the teacher's authority. Not knowing the names of all the students in the class, especially those from cultures other than one's own, is counter to inclusion, equality and diversity policies, but also demonstrates a teacher's lack of imaginative ability to connect across difference.

If teaching curricula where students are not sitting at desks, such as sport, then name stickers or name plaques at cooking stations in a training kitchen or beauty salon can be helpful. At the end of sessions teachers need to collect in name tabs and keep them for the following week. This is particularly important for teachers who have ten classes per week and cannot be expected to remember the names of all their students. In schools seating plans can be a major part of centralized, daily planning. In colleges seating plans are more usually the province of individual teachers. This can be achieved by numbering desks and giving students numbered tickets or group tasks on entry. Another method is to set the name tabs on desks so that they face the door and can be seen by students on entry. Students are placed where the teacher feels each person is best deployed for each session. The problems come when students refuse to co-operate and want to sit in friendship or ethnic groups. Each strategy has its own potential tensions, pressures and resistance; each resistance should be met by flexible, creative counter-strategies.

One key mode of control is ground rules which are best negotiated with students during the opening session (Gravells 2014). If democratically agreed and placed either on an easily available PowerPoint or classroom wall, then the teacher can point to the rule – e.g. 'NO MOBILES' – and say that the student who has infringed this rule was originally part of the decision to enforce it. This can work. However, the endemic use of mobiles in class is relentless. In some schools mobiles are banned, confiscated or put in a box at the beginning of a session. In colleges, these tactics are generally not possible. Students' personal identities are bound up with their phones. It is an assault on their person to take away their cell phone. It is also supposedly an adult environment where students need to contact a range of people outside college for medical or emergency, but sometimes personal, reasons. In many cases I have witnessed, students would rather fight teachers than relinquish their phone. Many students have more than one phone, so merely confiscating a phone does not solve the problem. Using phones as a research tool is one way of countering their use as an infinite extension of students' social lives. The slippage, however, into social media is often all too tempting.

Each lesson needs a scheme of work; lesson plan; meaningful activities; exciting, possibly digitally generated resources; points of interest for the whole class; a dynamic teacher; maybe student self-rating before and after teaching on students' perceptions of various activities, comprehension and/or enjoyment, plus discussions that will hopefully engage all students in the learning process. However, just because all these elements are present does not mean there might not be major disruption in the class. It is more unlikely that there will be problems, but awkward students can present their issues in the most perfect contexts. The perfect

Ofsted lesson (Beere 2012) requires the convenience of the perfect Ofsted class. Teachers can walk into classes exceptionally well-prepared, but can be faced with students kicking over desks, chatting, jeers and antagonism to the supposed authority of the teacher. Possibly worst of all, teachers might be faced with sheer indifference as if their arrival was a non-event.

The problem, challenge and ultimate fascination of being a teacher are that every class is different, but each teacher also has their own personality, energy, developed/developing skills, extrovert-introvert quotient and abilities to connect and communicate with diverse groups. It is impossible to legislate. However, I would recommend certain key strategies to be embedded at both macro and micro level beyond those which have already been discussed.

Recommendations for consideration

At a training level, in my view, all trainee teachers need to undergo a mandatory module or section of their PGCE/Cert Ed. course where behaviour management is the focus. In my research 90 per cent of trainees questioned wanted this (Lebor 2017).

The content of training should:

- Explore case study after case study where learning was resisted and how trainees could/should or might resolve these issues.
- Create role plays dealing with a range of extreme situations is a way of expanding trainees' psychological and emotional range.

In terms of management, despite challenges:

- Whole college policies need to be developed.
- Use identity badges.
- Apply college-wide monitoring systems for checking students across the institution.
- Managers need to adopt a supportive framework for ensuring staff can speak without fear of recrimination about negative events in their classrooms.
- Time should be given in staff meetings to discuss anything problematic that is happening each week in classrooms if necessary.
- Members of the teaching team should operate as support for anyone facing difficult classes.
- Managers should offer team-teaching as a way of showing 'the disruptive class' that the department all support one another.

Even the 'best' teachers can be timetabled to teach difficult classes. The isolation of individual teachers must stop!

Teachers need to be well-prepared with lesson plans, activities and resources. They also need to develop emotional resilience (Goleman 1999) and communication abilities to find that point of connection with each student. Teachers should demonstrate connection, interest and relationship, and model a spirit of enquiry through their questioning and engagement with students. Reversing power and turning students into teachers, conveying required information has a powerful effect on student learning. Teachers need to develop their voices, aligning their neck and head so they can be heard even in large and highly populated classrooms (Goyder 2012). Teachers might practise gestures in front of mirrors or through role play with colleagues. Teachers must develop flexibility in their personalities, so they can, with equanimity, encounter a wide range of behaviours. Teachers have the challenge to convey information and deliver the curriculum, but then the reward is the potential to transform many hundreds, if not thousands, of lives (Mezirow 2000).

Activities

Role plays to practise: Here are several scenarios with a range of possible, but not authoritative responses. Please feel free to adapt and extend. Discuss with other colleagues/trainees.

1 Helen refuses to open her file and carry out the class task.

- I need you to open your file.

- Are you ready yet to open your file?

- Helen why are you doing this qualification? Where do you hope it will lead?

- What is stopping you opening your file?

- What would you like to do on this topic, Helen?

2 James is disrespectful to you in the classroom. He says 'you can't teach me anything about x … You're younger than me … You know nothing.'

- What is your experience of x, James?

- James, where did you learn about x?

- Do you want to teach the next 10 minutes of the session, James?

- What is your evidence for saying that I know nothing about x?

3 Twenty students are chatting, on mobiles and not focused on the teacher when s/he enters the classroom.

- Can I have your attention please! (No one pays attention)

- Class, please!

- Thank you for your attention.

- We are starting the session in one minute (countdown on digital clock).

- Put on music to get attention or calm the class.

- This is your first task today (giving out worksheets).

- The reasons this class is important for your future careers are …

4 'I hate her. I'm not sitting next to her. She is disgusting!'

- You are not being respectful to one of your colleagues!

- How would you feel if someone said this about you?

- Why do you hate so much? What is hate?

- What are the good points about her/you?

- Is there any place you feel you can sit?

- This is discriminatory; I must ask you to step outside the classroom, so we can discuss *your* problems in more detail.

References

ATL (2016), *Education Staff Facing Physical Violence from Pupils*. Available online: https://www.atl.org.uk/media-office/2016/education-staff-facing-physical-violence-from-pupils.asp (accessed 15 April 2018).

Avis, J., Fisher, R., and Thompson, R. (2015), *Teaching in Lifelong Learning: A Guide to Theory and Practice*, Maidenhead: Open University Press.

Ball, S. (2003), 'The Teacher's Soul and the Terrors of Performativity', *Journal of Education Policy*, 18 (2): 215–228.

BBC (1998), 'Corporal Punishment Banned For All', 25 March. Available online: news.bbc.co.uk/2/hi/uk/politics/69478.stm (accessed 31 March 2016).

Beere, J. (2012), *The Perfect Ofsted Lesson*, Camarthen: Crown House Publishing.

Bennett, T. (2015), 'New Behaviour Tsar Tom Bennett's Top Ten Tips for Maintaining Classroom Discipline', *TES*. Available online: https://www.tes.com/news/school-news/breaking-views/new-behaviour-tsar-tom-bennetts-top-ten-tips-maintaining-classroom (accessed 31 March 2016).

British Educational Research Association (2018), *Ethical Guidelines for Educational Research*, 4th edn, London: BERA.

Cowley, S. (2014), *Getting the Buggers to Behave*, 5th edn, London: Bloomsbury Education.

DFE (2012), 'Pupil Behaviour in Schools in England', *DFE-RR218*. Available online: https://www.education.gov.uk/publications/ (accessed 31 March 2016).

Ecclestone, K. (2009), 'From Emotional and Psychological Well-Being to Character Education: Challenging Policy Discourses of Behavioural Science and "Vulnerability"', *Research Papers in Education*, 27 (4): 463–480.

Ellis, S., and Tod, J. (2014), *Promoting Behaviour for Learning in the Classroom: Effective Strategies, Personal Style and Professionalism*, London: Routledge.

Freire, P. (1972), *The Pedagogy of the Oppressed*, Harmondsworth: Penguin.

Goleman, D. (1999), *Working with Emotional Intelligence*, London: Bloomsbury.

Goyder, C. (2012), 'How to Voice Projection', *YouTube*. Available online: https://www.youtube.com/watch?v=ynmemxQicQk (accessed 31 March 2016).

Gravells, A., and Simpson, S. (2014), *The Certificate in Education and Training*, London: Sage.

Guardian (2017), 'Stabbed Teacher Ann Maguire's Inquest Will Not Hear Pupils' Evidence', *Guardian*, 14 August. Available online: https://www.theguardian.com/uk-news/2017/aug/14/stabbed-teacher-ann-maguire-inquest-will-not-hear-pupils-evidence (accessed 15 April 2018).

Hemmings, R. (1972), *Fifty Years of Freedom. A.S. Neill and the Evolution of the Summerhill Idea*, London: Allen & Unwin.

Hyland, T. (2006), 'Vocational Education and Training and the Therapeutic Turn', *Educational Studies*, 32 (3): 299–306.

Illich, I. (1971), *Deschooling Society*, New York: Harper & Row.

Knowles, M. (1975), *Self-Directed Learning. A Guide for Learners and Teachers*, Cambridge, Englewood Cliffs: Prentice Hall.

Kounin, J. (1997), *Discipline and Group Management in Classrooms*, New York: Holt, Rhinehart and Winston.

Lebor, M. (2000), 'One Strike and You're Out', *Guardian*, 17 April. Available online: https://www.theguardian.com/education/2000/feb/08/furthereducation.theguardian1 (accessed 15 April 2018).

Lebor, M. (2013), 'Class Wars: Initial Steps into the Fray', *Teaching In Lifelong Learning*, 5 (1): 21–31.

Lebor, M. (2014), 'War Stories; How Experienced Teachers Said They Responded to Disruptive Students in the Lifelong Learning Sector', *Teaching in Lifelong Learning: A Journal to Inform and Improve Practice*, 5 (2): 12–21.

Lebor, M. (2017), *Classroom Behaviour Management in the Post-School Sector: Student and Teacher Perspectives on the Battle against Being Educated*, London: Macmillan.

Mezirow, J. (2000), *Learning as Transformation: Critical Perspectives on a Theory in Progress*, San Francisco, CA: Jossey-Bass Inc.

Ofsted (2014), 'Below the Radar: Low Level Disruption in Classrooms'. Available online: https://www.gov.uk/government/publications/below-the-radar-low-level-disruption-in-the-countrys-classrooms (accessed 31 March 2016).

Ofsted (2006), *Improving Behaviour*, HMI 2377, London: Crown Copyright.

Parry, D., and Taubman, D. (2013), *UCU Whole College Behaviour Management: Final Report*, London: UCU.

Petty, G. (2014), *Teaching Today: A Practical Guide*, 5th edn, London: Oxford.

Rogers, B. (2015), *Classroom Behaviour*, 2nd edn, London: Sage.

UCU (2013), *Classroom Management: UCU Continuing Professional Development*. Available online: http://cpd.web.ucu.org.uk/files/2013/07/CPD-factsheet-6.pdf (accessed 15 April 2018).

Wallace, S. (2007), *Getting the Buggers Motivated in FE: Essential FE Toolkit*, London: Continuum.

Wallace, S. (2013), *Managing Behaviour in the Lifelong Learning Sector, 2nd edition*, Exeter: Sage.

Wallace, S. (2017), *Behaviour Management: Getting It Right in a Week*, St. Albans: Critical Publishing.

Wolf, A. (2011), *Wolf Review of 14–19 Vocational Education* (March), London: DfE.

Wong, H. (2009), *The First Day of School; How to Be an Effective Teacher*, California: HarryWong.

Yorkshire Evening Post (2014), 'Armed Police Called to Fistfight Near Leeds School!', *Yorkshire Evening Post*, 2 June. Available online: https://www.yorkshireeveningpost.co.uk/news/armed-police-called-to-fistfight-near-leeds-school-1-6650584 (accessed 15 April 2018).

4 A Critique of Common Current Approaches to Behaviour Management

SANDRA RENNIE

Introduction

This chapter will provide an exploration of behaviour management approaches as applied to a range of learning contexts primarily in the Vocational Education and Training (VET) sector. In the VET sector you will find mandated and reluctant learners; learners disillusioned and disaffected following poor school experiences; learners from families leading pressured and precarious lives; traumatized refugees and, on the positive side; groups of happy, contented leisure class students and many other variations and combinations of all ages, ability and experience. Consequently, behaviour management cannot be presented as 'a one size fits all' solution for all contexts. The following selection of behaviour approaches is based on a review of some of the current textbooks in use in teacher education, some practitioner research undertaken, a sampling of the issues and approaches commonly reported via the internet, the national press and other media and a review of approaches used by training providers of continuous professional development courses on behaviour management. Rather than being a totally randomized or systematized selection, the choice is based on the author's own humanist view of the purpose of education. To tease out the practical implications of the considered approaches, the author has also used her personal observations of teachers and of trainee teachers and reflections on her own teaching practice, and her participation in learning groups and lived experience. These personally observed anecdotes and strategies are kept anonymous to protect the privacy of teachers and others concerned.

There is an inherent contradiction in the idea of behaviour being 'managed' in a learning context. On the one hand, students need a comfortable and ordered environment to be able to hear the teacher, and they need it to be healthy and safe so they can practise the skills learned without injury to themselves or others. On the other hand, learning is about being able to take risks, being able to push the boundaries of established knowledge and to stretch our own abilities as learners. If we do not try new activities, ask new questions and take new risks, we are condemning students to becoming people who are trained to follow instructions, repeat back given information without necessarily understanding it and to be continuously reliant on a teacher/master/mistress to provide them with direction. These students become permanently stuck in the role of trainees rather than growing into active, creative and self-actualizing learners able to act on their own initiative and to freely work and cooperate with others. This directive approach is illustrated by a phrase I have heard from both teachers and students who have lost patience with quality assurance procedures, 'just tell me what to say and which box to complete on the form and I will do it', with the implication being that then they can get on with the real business of their lives as the concepts of 'quality' and 'education' have become an irrelevance.

The range and selection of behaviour approaches

As trainee teachers we learn from a range of disciplines when looking for approaches that could be applied to behaviour management in the classroom. Ideas sourced from the disciplines of Social Psychology, Sociology, Neuro-physiology, Management theory, and even Interior Design and Architecture can be considered relevant subjects for underpinning effective behaviour management. In the teacher education textbooks, at one end of the spectrum, theorists are quoted who focus on learning as a group activity and see good behaviour as a result of an effective understanding of group dynamics, and at the other end of the spectrum are theorists who focus on behaviour management as the business and responsibility of individuals. For example, managing group dynamics and promoting a positive classroom atmosphere are central to the approaches adopted by Canter (2010), Kounin (1970) and Cowley (2014). Canter (2010: 11) advocates 'assertive discipline' when he describes how teachers should develop an assertive 'voice' thus:

> When dealing with disruptive students, teachers with the voice will, in a calm, firm manner simply tell the students what they are to be doing and, if appropriate, the corrective actions (disciplinary consequences) they have chosen to receive by their behaviour.

Kounin's idea that an effective teacher requires 'withitness' is based on an understanding of the importance of group dynamics. The concept of 'withitness', as described by Ellis and Todd, 'represents the teacher's active awareness and monitoring of the multiple relationships that exist within the classroom' (Ellis and Todd 2009: 172). Cowley's view is also one which focuses on managing group relationships. She believes that constant, low-level disruptions in class causes stress for teachers, who already feel they are under pressure and overworked because of crowded classrooms and excessive paperwork. In response to this, Cowley proposes easily implemented tips for teachers like 'know what you expect from your students' and 'communicate it to them so that there are no ambiguities' and 'react to misbehaviour by suggesting positive alternatives' (Cowley 2014: 6).

There are theorists who adopt more individual-centred approaches by putting the responsibility for 'good behaviour' squarely on the shoulders of each student and each teacher. For example, to Hattie self-esteem is important and he advocates considering the many-stranded and overlapping concepts of 'self' that a learner may have which can lead to either 'self-efficacy' or 'self-handicapping'. To Hattie, as students we have chances to 'protect, present, preserve and promote so that we can "back ourselves", that is maintain our self-esteem' (Hattie 2014: 40). Bob Bates (2016) in his book *Learning Theories Simplified* has also given the example of Willingham, writing in 2009, whom he describes as a theorist, informed by cognitive science, who emphasizes the importance of teachers not overloading a learner with what is irrelevant and unimportant. Bates also includes Hare writing in 2003 in his list of behaviour management theorists. Hare is a psychologist who studies people who have 'psychopathic tendencies', and it is argued in these cases that the teacher needs to recognize and respond to such students appropriately (Bates 2016: 152–162). To individual-centred theorists like these the required student role is to follow instructions and exercise self-control and self-management. The teacher's role is to identify what needs to be done, give instructions and convey expectations that these will be followed. This list of individual-centred theorists and group-centred theorists, with some slight variations, is also commonly cited in other teacher education textbooks reviewed, for example, as in *Achieving Your Diploma in Education and Training* (Gould and Roffey-Barentsen 2014: 223–230).

Historical approaches still in common use

There is a backlog of established theories dating from as far back as the 1940s and 1950s and even earlier. These theories are still taught to trainee teachers and used as justification for teaching strategies by practising teachers, for example, Maslow's 'Hierarchy of Needs' (Maslow 1943) and Skinner's 'Behaviourism' (Skinner 1953) which were still commonly quoted by trainee teachers I encountered in my practitioner-based research – sometimes cited without the benefit of updates or more recent criticisms of them. These theories have been taken up by two or even three generations of teachers in the classroom. Their persistence may be because they seem to be 'common sense' theories that can be easily applied in a practical class management. For example:

> Learners who feel secure and free from anxiety, and experience a positive, inclusive learning environment are more likely to turn their attention towards learning. Managing the learning environment therefore plays a significant part in managing learners. (Gould and Roffey-Barentsen 2014: 216)

This quote seems to be a common-sense statement. However, generalizations like these are not always helpful in practice. Our knowledge of how the brain functions and how it changes over time is growing considerably in the light of functional magnetic resonance imaging (MRI) brain scans and other new techniques for assessing activity in the brain. Old, traditional psychological theories like Maslow's and Skinner's may prove to be mistaken or irrelevant. Maslow's hierarchy of needs advocates the provision of a safe environment for learning, but it now could be argued that too much safety prevents growth in neuroplasticity and thus damages students' learning potential. Similarly, Skinner's behaviourism underpins instructional approaches to education and we may argue that this directive approach does not stimulate growth in the brain's centres of creativity and innovation.

If a trainee teacher or education manager is researching behaviour theories on the internet, they will find that Skinner's ideas appear early in the internet search, partly because the word 'behaviourism' sounds like 'behaviour theories'. There is a similar issue with Maslow's 'Hierarchy of Needs', as many hundreds of images of Maslow's 'Hierarchy of Needs' can be found on the internet under a search of Google images. This may be a case of an accessible internet meme influencing the content of both teacher training and management training. The pyramid image of Maslow's 'Hierarchy of Needs' has 'physiological needs' needs at the base, then the image progresses up through higher levels past 'safety needs', up through 'social needs', then 'esteem needs' and finally topping off the pyramid at the 'need for self-actualization'. The teacher can easily use this pyramid image to help analyse the motivation behind their students' behaviour (Figure 4.1). For example, the new teacher could be asked to check to see if all their students' 'physiological needs' have been met. This is very relevant if any of your students have missed breakfast or have hangovers and require water to drink, or it is in the middle of the month of Ramadan and some of your students have been fasting and missing their sleep; however, it is only ever a partial explanation of disruptive behaviour.

Social and esteem needs, as described by Maslow, may be particularly relevant in a classroom where there is a mix of both young and old students, rich and poor, physically advantaged and physically disadvantaged. Class groups easily split up into cliques on social lines and those from the minority social class may find themselves excluded from conversations, marginalized and their lifestyles denigrated in discussions. Thus, a working-class student in a largely middle-class group may find themselves excluded from social groups or they may find their lifestyle or dress cause them to be the butt of jokes or vice versa. Some students' past experiences of studying were in crowded classrooms where they would avoid drawing attention to themselves in the way they stood, the clothes they wore or the way they talked as this would be described as 'asking for trouble', from their peers. These students will have different expectations of appropriate behaviour to other students who have been encouraged to value difference, encouraged to stand out from the crowd and who believe that 'if you want to get ahead, get a hat'. The gay student in a class where the culture is heteronormative may feel isolated and ignored and unable to participate in discussions about families or personal relationships. The person who is embarrassed or ashamed of their dyslexia may choose to become the 'class clown' to draw attention away from their learning difficulty. People who have even mild forms of autism or other types of neuro-diversity may find it difficult to socialize and hence become the victim of covert bullying and social exclusion. Undercurrents of threats to learners' 'social needs' and 'esteem needs' exist in every classroom and the teacher's job is to spot these threats and deal with

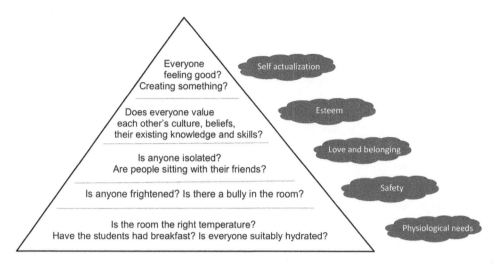

Figure 4.1 *Questions for teachers to ask themselves – based on Maslow's Hierarchy of Needs (1943).*

them before they bubble up to the surface and become a disruption to the constructive learning atmosphere.

B.F. Skinner's Theory of Operant Conditioning (1953) is also viewed a 'common-sense' theory and is ubiquitous on the internet. The advice promoted is to issue rewards for 'good' behaviour and 'negative consequences' (punishments) for 'bad' behaviour and to be consistent and even-handed when you do this. This theory of reward and punishment underpins the idea of 'tough love' promoted via *Teachers TV* and the national press over the last decade (for example Revell 2005). Furthermore, school students and others were encouraged to develop 'character and resilience' so they could learn to accept and respond to any negative consequences and disappointments and not, for example, just drop out of their education when challenged by their college to behave in a seemly way. The cross-party parliamentary 'Character and Resilience Manifesto' as reviewed by Howse (2014) argues that 'more importance should be given to the development of "character and resilience"'. It says schools should make it part of their 'core business' to nurture 'self-belief, perseverance and ability to bounce back from set-backs' (in reference to pupils). The room in a school set aside for 'time out', the exclusion of disruptive students from rewarding activities and the implementation of teacher-initiated punishments are all logical conclusions to this approach. This sounds like practical advice but to some teachers the strategy seems to emanate more from a management desire to control, corral and categorize students rather than to ensure that all, without exception, fulfil their educational potential.

Albert Bandura is extensively cited in searches. In *Simply Psychology* (Macleod 2016) he is described as stressing the importance of observational learning, imitation and modelling. Teachers 'model' behaviour and their students, either consciously or unconsciously, copy that behaviour. If this is further reinforced by rewards and other positive or negative outcomes, the behaviour becomes an established pattern in the student. If a teacher arrives late to a lesson, then the students would perceive that as acceptable. If the teacher decries the college paperwork as unnecessary and 'just something required of management', then the student has learned that it is considered reasonable to waste the time scheduled for learning in performing unnecessary tasks for those in positions of power.

Continuing professional development approaches

Education training consultancies provide one-off training and support as part of in-service teacher training and continuous professional development (CPD). Many of them present themselves as authoritative experts and espouse a chosen approach that can be easily covered in a one-day training session. For example, they provide advice on how to set ground rules in the beginning and stick to them or how to provide non-violent crisis intervention. Some advertise that they conduct behaviour audits or advocate a whole-institutional or whole-team approach. Others may specialize in supporting staff working with students on the autism spectrum or with students who have been described as having Attention Deficit and Hyperactivity Disorder (ADHD). There are many blog posts on the internet, placed by private training providers, which offer practical advice to teachers to encourage their participation in CPD programmes, for example Paul Dix's post for *The Guardian* (2012) which makes suggestions like 'stop ignoring good behaviour' and offers 'top tips' for newly qualified teachers. These must be treated cautiously as they are commercial organizations and blogs are useful for practitioner opinion, but they are not necessarily reviewed.

Practitioner insights on disruptive students

In the school sector the issue of teachers facing disruptions in classes from pupils has led to the government appointment of the so-called behaviour tsar Tom Bennett in June 2015 by the then Schools Minister, Nick Gibb. This 'ask the expert approach' initially focused on the use of smart-phones in schools and the issue of 'low-level disruption'. Tom Bennett has provided 'ten top tips' for dealing with behaviour management, most of which follow this 'tough love' approach and are not always relevant for teaching adults. As an experienced adult educator my own advice is – don't follow his tip for 'contacting the parents' or apply it to one of your older teenagers or adult students, and don't try arbitrarily removing mobile phones from adults. The problem with this 'ask the expert' approach is that it does not consider that the expert's tip cannot be relied to be transferrable to other spheres of experience in education. If a student is banging her head on the desk and thus disrupting the class and a trainee teacher wants to develop a strategy to deal with this incident and furthermore desires that their strategy should be informed by theory, then as a behaviourist and a believer in 'tough love', they need only to focus on the behaviour, not on the student, and instead issue rewards and sanctions until the behaviour ceases. This form of social conditioning, or brain-washing as it could be more unkindly called, may be effective in keeping a classroom free from disruptions so that the other, less troubled, students can learn. However, it could hardly be called inclusive as it neglects to deal with any personal and social barriers to learning or to tackle the negative experiences many teenage and adult learners may have had of education previously.

Modelling

Some teachers present their lives or their values as ideal models and expect their students to follow that model. A practical skills teacher started her first session with:

> Don't tell me you haven't got time to do your assignments. I am running three contracts, assessing students all over the country, I have a family and I'm studying for a degree as well. So, excuses about lack of time won't wash with me!

For work-based training and apprenticeships this is a common approach to managing behaviour. The teacher (or more commonly, the trainer) is presented as the 'master' of their craft and apprentices are considered as persons expected to copy and learn from the behaviour and the 'professionalism' modelled by this master craftsperson. The trainer would say they had the authority to demand this by their qualifications, skills and their work experience. Their trainees and apprentices are thus expected to unquestioningly accept and copy their 'master' teacher's model of behaviour.

Authority

While carrying out a research project on behaviour management in 2015 (unpublished) I questioned thirty trainee teachers about their worries and concerns while they were part way through their teaching practice. One worry expressed by several of them was they felt they were not seen as authoritative because of their age. Interestingly this applied to both young and old trainee teachers. Possessing authority and 'effective leadership' is promoted as a prerequisite for having an attentive and engaged group of learners. On the internet there are advice videos and courses available, for example informed by neuro-linguistic programming (NLP) (Elston 2018), telling you how to stand, how to sit and what sentences and phrases to use that exude authority and leadership. However, the appearance of authority is not the same quality as possessing real authority, and fake authority can be easily detected and challenged by students. Authority can be described as having three facets: first, a confidence that is a result of a combining a deep, personal knowledge of a subject; secondly, a public recognition that we possess this knowledge and; thirdly, an ability to recognize our limitations and to learn from our experiences. To summarize, it could be said that to possess the virtue of authority we need knowledge, qualifications and humility. Authority is not solely a function of age or even length of experience. If I have had forty years of experience which entailed me repeating the same mistakes each year forty times, then I am no more authoritative than a newly qualified teacher. Teachers who have been able to reflect regularly on their teaching practice with a mentor may find it easier to develop this authoritative persona. Teachers who have made efforts to keep up-to-date with innovations in information technology and the use of social media will also have confidence in the currency of their knowledge and thence more authority when teaching. Nothing undermines authority more than when an over-confident teacher blusters, bluffs and busks their way through the subject content.

Values

The very term 'behaviour management' implies that the person exhibiting the behaviour needs to be controlled and that their 'behaviour' is itself intrinsically harmful. I would suggest that we need to consider that deviant or aberrant behaviour exhibited by our students may well be a valuable sign that there are new things to be learned. This could be new understandings about the teacher, about the other students and about the social needs of others or about our own physiological functioning. Observing disruptive behaviour and participating in disruptive behaviour can be a learning opportunity. As a humanist I would argue that when we focus on controlling behaviour rather than first understanding it, we lose sight of the aim of education which, in my view, should be to draw out a love of learning for its own sake and to encourage questions as well as answers.

Faith-based schools present a different approach to education values and behaviour management. On the one hand, having a coherent and homogenous set of values governing a college or school may promote 'good', (that is 'unchallenging') behaviour in the students but, on the other hand, faith-based educational institutions are not guaranteed to produce autonomous, self-actualized, educated adults. Richard Pring (2005) has suggested that arguments for and against faith-based schools need to address 'educational aims and the promotion of a valued form of life, the autonomy of the child and the promotion of a particular creed and indoctrination and notions of rationality' (Pring 2005: 11). Islamic, Jewish and other faith-based schools often receive praise for their behaviour management in Ofsted reports, so we should consider what can be learned from their perspective on behaviour management approaches, while at the same time being mindful of the risk of indoctrination dominating over education.

I recently had teaching experiences within four different Islamic education institutions both in a school and a college type of environment. These institutions had been inspected and had each received positive feedback comments for their behaviour management. There are many possible reasons for this apart from the fact they were categorized as faith-based schools: it may be skilled behaviour management by the teachers; the homogenous culture among the students; the strong belief in the status; and respect due to teachers; or, it may be that there was a fully engaged community living physically nearby with parents and grandparents, other relatives and community leaders; as well as the teachers who were tasked with moderating behaviour. If you misbehaved one day, everyone (and everyone's auntie) would soon get to hear about it. Similarly, if you were treated unfairly there would be discussions about it in the street, complaints would be made and follow-up action would be instigated.

Social background

As teachers, our backgrounds, cultures and previous learning experiences help us construct our expectations of what is a positive and effective learning environment. They determine how we respond to physical space, to the movement and the sounds within the classroom, and they influence whatever rules and conventions we expect people to follow. These expectations are partly determined by our home background or social class as well as being a result of our personal predilections. The environment of your childhood can create a sense of physical confidence and entitlement in those who have been brought up in spacious homes, with gardens to run about in and who have attended schools with large playgrounds and small class numbers. I attended a single-sex school where class sizes were no bigger than twenty pupils and so I expected to have space to move about in, to feel comfortable when on stage and to some students I may have seemed aggressive or over-dramatic in my gestures. There is a different backstory for a trainee teacher whose school experience was in a crowded classroom of forty-plus children who grew up living in a flat where even the smallest noise affected the neighbours. Levels of generally acceptable noise can vary with age and disability too. When I was younger I preferred to work with background music; now I am older I find this very distracting and it interferes with my hearing. My autistic friend requires sound-muffling headphones if she is participating in learning in a noisy environment. Some teachers and students value the creative buzz of a noisy environment and others find silence essential for concentrated learning.

Policies and regulations can in this way be a secret weapon on the side of the management and, by implication, on the side of the teachers. They are 'secret' because even though policies are all officially published, their details are better understood by managers and teachers than by students. Some colleges attempt to be more open by carrying out comprehension tests and quizzes on the contents of a student handbook before asking students to sign learning contracts which cover their agreement to certain behaviour standards. If signing a behaviour contract were a free choice and if the students concerned had both the skills and authority to influence the shape of the terms of the behaviour contract, this approach could be categorized as a liberal and democratic approach. However, in practice where behaviour contracts or student learning agreements are in use there is generally no choice in the matter and they are applied equally to all as a prerequisite for the person starting college. Some students cannot understand the legal language of the rules; for example those with literacy skills below level 2 on the UK Qualification and Credit Framework will struggle to comprehend fully. Applicants must sign the agreement if they wish to become students and gain a qualification and many students agree to do so using the same reasoning as when they tick and agree to the 'terms and conditions' of a piece of software they buy online. They have not read the conditions, but they know they must tick the box to access the service needed. This is not a liberal approach; this is a compliance approach informed by a risk-averse management and as such it diminishes the respect and authority that students have for formal agreements, contracts and the law in general. In these circumstances it becomes a rational response for students to develop an instrumental approach to their education and to view cheating and plagiarism as acceptable as long as you do not get caught – because all that matters is that you achieve the necessary qualifications. They are following the ethics and behaviour examples modelled by their education managers and teachers who have required signatures and dates on these agreements but have not required their understanding or informed and freely given consent.

Motivation

My own college teaching experiences consisted of several years teaching well-motivated, bilingual adults in community language classes and several years running staff development courses for mandated participants. Students in the first category were easy to engage as they started with a culturally rooted respect for the role and status of a teacher. The mandated participants on staff development courses were, on the other hand, the most difficult to engage as they were reluctant learners who had been sent on these courses by their managers and some of them initially perceived their participation as a box-ticking exercise. Contrary to expectations, the most disruptive groups I have ever experienced in my whole teaching career were not the groups of 16–18-year-old unemployed youths learning 'life skills' or the adults with learning difficulties, they were in fact groups of qualified teachers attending courses that they did not wish to attend. Compulsory education courses are resisted both actively and passively by participants especially when they are perceived as indoctrination. Many such courses include topics required by managers as a result of policy innovations, for example: courses on inclusion and diversity; health and safety; safeguarding; data protection; 'prevent' policy; and (ironically) behaviour management itself. When education is perceived as indoctrination then it performs the opposite function of Maslow's highest human need of 'self-actualization'; it tends to destroy and negate any concept of self, any sense of freedom or independent agency. No wonder these professional teachers chose to behave in an 'unprofessional' manner.

We cannot hope for agreement and compliance with the managerialist approach to the regulation of behaviour unless it becomes established as custom and practice within the culture of the organization. On reflection it is hard to conjure up an example of an education organization, large or small, where the teachers and students regularly and routinely follow all the policies as laid out in their student handbooks and student learning agreements. Just as we can only have policing with consent, so we can only have institutional rule-following provided we have the active, informed consent of all.

Conclusion

In education we have a lot to learn from observing other behaviour management approaches, but we must be careful to not just copy what they do in practice but also ask how well they have succeeded and why. Furthermore, we need to consider how far we can generalize from the success of practices when they have only previously been carried out in specific localities or specific contexts with specific students. We need to ask whether the approaches advocated by 'authoritative' specialists are transferable and, if so, for what pedagogical reasons have they been chosen. Academic theorists can help us identify and respond to patterns occurring in a classroom, but the practical behaviour management approaches we eventually choose to use are more likely to be influenced by what seems doable in the circumstances or by tips we have picked up from teaching colleagues, managers or CPD courses. It is important not just to focus solely on the group dynamics or on the actions of individuals as both factors can affect the learning outcomes and behaviour within the classroom. As teachers we are influenced by our own life experiences and previous schooling as well as by our beliefs, values and predilections, so we need to be aware of these when making judgements about the behaviour of our students and our colleagues. In a climate of constant audit, informed and governed by changing education policies, education management has become more and more risk-averse. A liberal education approach to teaching and learning requires a certain amount of reflection and risk-taking to take place, otherwise what happens in the classroom becomes simply training and instruction using the stick and carrot of positive and negative consequences. A risk-averse and controlling approach to behaviour management may stifle creative, effective and transferrable learning. Those who espouse a more liberal approach to education may ultimately have to accept that, although behaviour in the classroom can be planned for, it cannot necessarily accurately be predicted. In conclusion, as well as being informed of the range of behaviour management approaches available to choose from, teachers need to learn the skills and habits of improvising behaviour management and to develop these habits based on the values they wish to promote.

Activities

1 Describe your own educational background. How different is it from your current students?

2 Do you consider yourself to be an authoritative teacher? How?

3 Can you envisage an occasion when you would choose not to follow the organization's rules? What would it look like?

References

Bates, B. (2016), *Learning Theories Simplified*, London: Sage.

Canter, L. (2010), *Assertive Discipline: Positive Behavior Management for Today's Classroom*, 4th edn, Bloomington, IN: Solution Tree Press.

Cowley, S. (2014), *Getting the Buggers to Behave*, 5th edn, London: Bloomsbury.

Dix, P. (2012), 'How to Go from "Good" to "Outstanding"', *The Guardian*, 23 April. Available online: https://www.theguardian.com/profile/paul-dix (accessed 9 July 2018).

Ellis, S., and Todd, J. (2009), *Behaviour for Learning: Proactive Approaches to Behaviour Management*, Oxon: Routledge.

Elston, T. (n.d.), 'How can Neuro-Linguistic Programming Help with Leadership and Development', *Neuro-Linguistic Programming World*. Available online: https://www.nlpworld. co.uk/how-can-neuro-linguistic-programming-help-with-leadership-and-development/ (accessed 2 May 2018).

Elston, T.(2018), https://www.youtube.com/user/terryelston/videos (accessed 8 November 2018)

Gibb, N. MP (2015), *Impact of Smartphones on Behaviour in Lessons to Be Reviewed*, DfE, 13 September. Available online: https://www.gov.uk/government/news/impact-of-smartphones-on-behaviour-in-lessons-to-be-reviewed (accessed 26 April 2018).

Gould, J., and Roffey- Barentsen, J. (2014), *Achieving Your Diploma in Education and Training*, London: Sage.

Hare, R.D. (2003), *The Psychopathic Checklist*, 2nd edn, Toronto: Multi Health Systems.

Hattie, J. (2014), *Visible Learning for Teachers*, London: Routledge.

Holden, C. (2016), 'Policy and Procedure in Behaviour Management Part 2', *Society for Education and Training*. Available online: https://set.et-foundation.co.uk/news-events/blogs-and-articles/blogs/policy-and-procedure-in-behaviour-management-part-two/ (accessed 25 April 2018).

Holden, C. (2015), *The Third Pillar of Behaviour Management*. Available online: http://www. chrisholdenonline.com/blog/the-third-pillar-of-behaviour-management (accessed 13 July 2018).

Howse, P. (2014), 'Schools Urged to Promote Character and Resilience', *BBC*, 11 February. Available online: http://www.bbc.co.uk/news/education-26118581 (accessed 25 April 2018).

Kounin, J.S. (1970), *Discipline and Group Management in Classrooms*, New York: Holt, Reinhart and Winston.

Macleod, S. (2016), 'Bandura – Social Learning Theory', *Simply Psychology*. Available online: https://www.simplypsychology.org/bandura.html (accessed 1 July 2018).

Maslow, A. [1943] (2013), *A Theory of Human Motivation*, reprint, USA: Martino Publishing.

Revell, P. (2005), 'Tough Love', *The Guardian*, 25 October. Available online: https://www.theguardian.com/education/2005/oct/25/pupilbehaviour.classroomviolence (accessed 25 April 2018).

Pring, R. (2005), 'Faith Schools: Can They Be Justified', in R. Gardner, J. Cairns and D. Lawton (eds), *Faith Schools: Consensus or Conflict?*, 51–60, London: Routledge.

Skinner, B.F. (1953), *Science and Human Behaviour*, USA: The Macmillan Co.

Willingham, D. (2009), *Why Don't Students Like School?*, San Francisco, CA: Jossey Bass.

5 Affirmative Mental Health Leadership

LOU MYCROFT

The purpose of this chapter

This chapter is designed to be iconoclastic, so be warned. Trawling through the 'offcuts' of a national research project around mental health and education[1] as a member of the 'MHFE Crowd',[2] the author, a former public health specialist and teacher educator, was privileged to observe educators grappling in some cases with their own mental well-being alongside supporting (adult) students with mild to moderate mental health problems. This sparked an interest in affirmative mental health leadership for educators, enacted through the design, delivery and evaluation of professional development training,[3] reading, research and endless dialogue: a *bricolage* (Greet 2017) of praxis. The chapter offers some background to the unprecedented mental health and well-being challenges currently facing UK educators and students[4] and impacting on classroom behaviours. It offers an affirmative mental health pedagogy based on the *Thinking Environment* (Kline 2009) paradox of 'Freedom Needs Boundaries'; six propositions with the potential to reimagine the culture of UK state education to address a crisis of mental ill-health.

Context: UK further education in 2018

As many have written elsewhere (see, for example, Daley et al. 2015 and 2017 and both Robinson (Chapter 1) and Bennett (Chapter 2) in this volume), the policy drift in state-

---

[1]Funded through the £20 million Department for Education (DfE) initiative announced in the 2014 Autumn Statement, the Community Learning Mental Health research project tested out whether short, part-time community learning courses help people develop strategies to manage their mild to moderate mental health problems (like stress, worry, anxiety and depression). At the time of writing, the research has yet to report.
[2]The MHFE Crowd comprises educators who co-curate the website www.mhfe.org.uk and who were involved at various times and in various ways during the CLMH research, above.
[3]'Breaking the Rules'.
[4]For the purposes of clarity, 'educator' is used to describe anyone in a teaching, guidance and/or learning support role and 'student' to describe anyone in a learning role, whether adult, young person or child.

funded further education (FE) over the past twenty years has been towards the skills training of economically productive human resources, to feed the country's economic growth; despite this, the sector is chronically underfunded, with a consequential impact on the workload and contractual precarity of staff. The language, structure and culture of FE have shaped themselves to policy and, following the raising of the school-leaving age (in England at least), which saw huge numbers of 16–18-year-olds enter FE from 2013 onwards, many FE colleges have become huge, visible and multi-academized, foregrounded in national discourse to some extent (although FE remains 'the poor sister') due to influential representation from the Association of Colleges, while other adult learning contexts are overlooked. Adults continue to learn in communities, in prisons, on the job, in private training companies, in third sector organizations, on weekends away, in books and online, self-funded and state-funded and will continue to do so even as access pipelines dry up and affordability wanes.

Introduction – a bowerbird approach

The material of story mostly arises from the detritus of the mundane.

GREET 2017: 186

In a world of evidence-based practice, defined compellingly broadly by Jones (2016) and more narrowly by others (Hammersley 2001), ethnography and other observational practices retain an honourable foothold (Hastrup 1990). This chapter is presented as a bricolage (Greet 2017), or perhaps more colourfully as 'bowerbirding', a concept used by (female) Antipodean researchers to describe a method of 'selection, collection, curation and display' (Greet 2017: 192). The (male) bowerbird, with its bright blue eye, collects bright blue objects with which to thematically decorate its nest. Thus, my 'bright blue eye' selects some pieces of evidence and rejects others, relying on a reflexive, personal ethics to aim not for objectivity, but for transparent curation. My inconsistent, but at times intensive, immersion in the Community Learning Mental Health (CLMH) project and my dual professionalism as a public health specialist and teacher educator inform the evidence presented and my personal standpoint. As an observer and bowerbird, I aim for trustworthiness and make no claim to absolute 'truth'. I believe this process of curation can provide new perspectives on the mundane:

Writers are perverse. They do not accept the world at face value. They insist on rending the social fabric, to inspect the warp and weave, inverting the usual, turning things on their heads, interrogating [what Jane Austen termed] life's 'busy nothings'.

(Greet 2017: 187)

The chapter assumes that we all have 'mental health' and rejects the notion that anyone is immune to mental *ill*-health.

Context: mental ill-health and the crisis in 'behaviour'

Mental ill-health, the 'madwoman in the attic' (Gilbert and Gubar 2000) and forever the NHS's underfunded 'Cinderella Service' (Tingle 2017), has been pushed to the point of renaissance – at least in public discourse – by the desperate rise in mental health morbidity in the UK[5] (DoH/DfE 2017; Thorley 2017). The impact on schools, universities and 'lifelong learning' (a term embraced by New Labour in the 1990s, which largely failed to embrace the unparalleled diversity of non-higher adult education) is reverberating through the axioms of the state education system (Thorley 2017).

Educators find themselves at the apex of not only this national disgrace/crisis but also the demands of their own personal mental well-being, as workloads squeeze and contracts wobble (Education Support Partnership 2017). This chapter presents a brief argument for why teacher education (including continuing professional development) needs to fundamentally redesign its offer for educators who are squeezed between these dual pressures. In the meantime, it makes practical, workable suggestions for affirmative mental health practice in the classroom, which offer opportunities to address the impact of mental ill-health on learning and teaching behaviours.

As Natasha Devon, former mental health 'tsar' for schools (dramatically ghosted from post after nine months), writes:

> In our complex and often toxic culture, there is so much pressure for the adults who are guiding young people to be 'perfect'.
>
> (Devon and Crilly 2015: 2)

This holds equally true for those of us working with adults. In education, the additional spectre of Ofsted inspection and its attendant compliances drive a perfectionist culture which is profoundly damaging to health and well-being. Brown (2015) describes the detrimental impact of perfectionism, reducing the courage of individuals to express vulnerability and admit to mistakes. In organizations, this leads to blame, (self) shame, illness and exhaustion; risk-averse cultures of compliance where creativity and innovation and their potential for mistake-making which might be theoretically welcomed as a nod to the rapidly changing world outside but are, in practice, feared.

In recent research conducted by Leeds Beckett University, teachers identified the negative impact of their own mental ill-health on students' progress (Teachwire 2018). Interestingly, most teachers felt their ability to assess learning,[6] drummed into them for two

---

[5]Particularly, but not exclusively, among young people and children. Not surprisingly mental ill-health is particularly prevalent in marginalized groups (DoH/DfE 2017).

[6]In the face of compelling evidence that written assessment is 'the straw that breaks the camel's back' in terms of teacher workload, the Education Endowment Foundation (Elliott et al. 2016) found that evidence of the effectiveness of written marking was low. They recommended further research to enable teachers (and organizations) to make informed decisions about how to use their time.

decades as the most essential element of education, was affected least; what did impact on classroom practice was their (lack of) physical energy, the ability to opportunistically question, probe and challenge – and creativity.[7] They could carry out certain functional tasks under the weight of mental and physical exhaustion – up to a point – but not opportunistic or creative ones.

In 2016, 50,000 qualified teachers left the state schools sector and a crisis in recruitment looms (National Education Union 2018). Under the 'exam factory' conditions of UK state education (Coffield and Williamson 2011), with the mental health of educators and students fraying, relationships break down. Influential behaviour practitioner Paul Dix argues:

> In behaviour management, culture eats strategy for breakfast. Getting the right culture is pivotal. With the right culture, the strategies that are used become less important. The culture is set by the way that adults[8] behave.

> (Dix 2017: 2)

Dix and many other behaviour specialists call for restorative approaches to behaviour 'management'. Each of the strategies detailed towards the end of this chapter focuses on methods by which educators can lead cultural change in learning environments, for the promotion of everyone's mental well-being.

The challenge to teacher education

There is little evidence that initial teacher education is stepping-up to the plate with this, or other twenty-first-century challenges, such as training teachers for a post-colonial world (Bhopal and Rhamie 2014). That's not to say that there aren't pockets of excellent practice, in the face of often insurmountable pressure; initial teacher education – particularly the academic study of pedagogy – has been undermined philosophically and practically in recent years (Iredale 2018), with continuing professional development (CPD) shifting from the traditional academic paradigm of universities to the practical 'what works' approach of training agencies directly funded by the state.

This is not an attack on teacher education, rather a call to arms which echoes the campaigning spirit of the *Dancing Princess* volumes (Daley et al. 2015, 2017), an exhortation to educators to determine education's direction of travel. If the future of teacher education is left only in the hands of policy-makers, it will continue to wither. The crisis in mental health faced by educators and students needs teacher education to become a site of struggle for a radically reworked and decolonized curriculum – no matter what delivery

---

[7] 'Schools kill creativity' (Robinson 2014) for educators as well as students, it seems.
[8] This includes adults who work with other adults in a non-infantilizing way in further, community, offender, skills, higher and other manifestations of adult education.

model – which includes all our myriad diversities, including neurodiversity and mental health. The propositions, below, are offered in the spirit of a starting point for such a reimagining.

Neurodiversity

The campaigning movement of neurodiversity which was initially led by autistic people is an additional element in a complex and ill-thought-out mix of educational assumptions, often wrapped up under the umbrella of SEND (special education needs and disability). A genuinely protective desire to provide diagnostic labels as a starting point for additional learning support has benefitted many down the years and should not be discounted. However, the neurodiversity paradigm, although hotly contested, lines up alongside other civil rights movements to proactively campaign for assumptions of deficit to be overturned.

In the way that classrooms are unspokenly white (Bhopal 2018), they are also unspokenly neurotypical (Armstrong 2011). Armstrong draws on the metaphor of the brain as an ecosystem to make a compelling point that there is no such thing as a 'normal' brain against which every other brain is remedial. He recognizes social bias, how it changes over time and how it is reflected in the way society views, for example, dyslexia (very differently from when agrarian societies did not rely on the written word). He calls not for the removal of labelling but for the recognition of neurotypical privilege and the rethinking of diagnostic labels in terms of strengths, mediated and amplified in some cases by the affordances of digital technology, such as an iPhone, as an organizing tool for someone with ADHD. Imagine a classroom where that phone is not put away and,

> instead of always having to adapt to a static, fixed or 'normal' environment, it's
> possible for [neurodivergent people] to alter the environment to match the needs
> of their own unique brains. In this way, they can be more of who they really are.
> (Armstrong 2011: 17–18)

Armstrong points out a threefold rise in the categories of psychiatric illness in the second half of the twentieth century (2011: 3). His challenge is this: what if we didn't pathologize neurodiversity (and mental ill-health) in the way that we do? What might that look like, for education?

Restorative practices

When neurodiversity and mental well-being are foregrounded for all the actors in a learning environment, the onus is on the teacher to take a lead in building relationships which foster respect. Mirsky (2007: 6) describes a school intervention, where relationship work came second to 'restorative' content. According to the head teacher:

We made a critical error; we addressed the content of the program, not relationships between teachers and students. And from the first day, the program was as close to disaster as you can imagine. Rebelling against the lack of structure, unmotivated kids roamed the building, their behavior rude and belligerent. Teachers turned on each other, frustrated and upset.

Freedom needs boundaries, and boundaries are not the same as rules. Dix (2017) contends that checklists of behaviour management rules, subject to the whims of politicians and fashionable 'drive-by' training, are no substitute for effective pastoral care. Mirsky's research (2007: 6) found that restorative practices have a positive effect on academic performance:

> You cannot separate behavior from academics. When students feel good and safe and have solid relationships with teachers, their academic performance improves.

According to Mirsky, the link between educator and student well-being is that teachers have to take care of themselves (as a team) before they can create learning environments that empower students. Written simply, that seems like a no-brainer, yet there are powerful advocates for rules-based 'no tolerance' approaches to classroom behaviour. Unhelpfully, the pendulum of public educational discourse often swings between two 'extremes': punishing bad behaviour and trying to understand its causes. A closer, more nuanced reading of the landscape, with better listening on both sides rather than a 'fetish of assertion' (Williams 2002) might open up new thinking spaces to reimagine what an affirmative mental health approach to the education of all ages might be.

Breaking the rules

About halfway through the CLMH project, it became clear that distributed leadership was happening on a grand scale, as individuals began to take a lead in upskilling their organizations around affirmative mental health development. The project leads had broken through an FE given[9] that students, not educators, were inevitably the people who needed mental health support. This shift from 'them' to 'all of us' coincided with a mandatory leadership programme, 'Breaking the Rules', which took as its starting point Wilson's (2014) concept of the anti-heroic leader, in order to identify, deconstruct and rebuild some of the axiomatic thinking with which education is riddled.

Resistance to change haunted the CLMH project and 'Breaking the Rules' was only partially successful in getting beyond this; successful, that is, in some cases and not in others. Ironically, adult education is an utterly meme-ified space: it is impossible to find

---

[9] A generalization, which certainly held true in most cases.

a classroom or corridor which does not talk the language of transformation, diversity and well-being on its walls.

The reality of practice is different. The rise of technocratic teaching practices, particularly in the US Charter Schools movement (as an example), offers educators a panacea in difficult times; do *this* activity and you will get *that* result. Education theory has been reduced to 'Haynes Manual' instruction guides which, grounded in behaviourist approaches, ignore the complexity of human interactions and standardize teaching practice in the same way that learning is becoming standardized for children. Practices such as SLANT (Sit up, Lean Forward, Ask and Answer questions, Nod your head and Track the teacher) are becoming commonplace within UK classrooms and high-fiving 'tips and techniques' protocol sets such as Lemov's 'Teach Like a Champion' (2010) are scrutinized by busy educators wanting a quick overhaul.

'Breaking the Rules' was frustratingly (for some) different, reintroducing the need to understand, as an educator/leader, *why* you do what you do: no quick fixes but patient reflexivity, focusing on organizational change which builds autonomy and trust. Working together across aspects of disagreement using pro-social approaches, we questioned whether compliance was really the hallmark of a 'good' student (or educator) and battered down some of education's taken-for-granted icons: namely grit, resilience and the lost subtleties of Dweck's sensible 'growth mindset' theory (2017), which, a decade after publication, was being used as the educational equivalent of the mental health clichè 'pull yourself together': work harder! Many of the affirmative mental health projects that came out of 'Breaking the Rules' used digital to breach the 'fourth wall' of the classroom and moved into fresher dialogic spaces.

Tzviel Rofé, a writer and mental health activist, works with story metaphors to broker communication when 'the gap in knowledge and experience between the communicators is too large'. His story of 'Splinters in a Small Box' (Rofé 2009: 473) illustrates what happened when he bridged this gap through talking with health professionals about his experiences of mental ill-health. Pedagogies, like stories, can span perspectives, identities and power-differentials.

Affirmative mental health pedagogy – six propositions

This chapter proposes a pedagogy of six propositions, each of which is built on a pro-social approach.[10] The intention is to enact a process which honours the disability activist maxim 'Nothing About Us without Us' (Warner 1998) by learning from the lived experience of educators and students on the CLMH project and elsewhere. Although as we have seen the

---

[10]Pro-social pedagogies are facilitation techniques which build community. They do not replace the knowledge component of an educator's role; rather they help create the conditions in which new knowledge can be processed and applied.

autonomy of educators has been eroded in many ways, it is hoped that each proposition falls within an educator's locus of control, with a reasonable expectation of support from the organization. As we affirmed during 'Breaking the Rules' and despite open doors, unshaded windows and learning walks, the classroom is still a space where educator and student can participate in an engaged pedagogy (hooks 1994: 15), where educators are 'actively committed to a process of self-actualization that promotes their own well-being if they are to teach in a manner that empowers students'.

Teaching with ease

Easier said than done, you might think, in the 'exam factory' environments which characterize UK state education. Yet creating the conditions for people – including the educator – to do their best thinking can save time and costly diversions.

Kline's (2009) work describes *Thinking Environment* processes, which provide a framework for learning interventions such as teaching, coaching and mentoring. A thinking round, which brings everyone present into the room, introduces an element of ease and even silence which is anathema to the technocratic classroom:

> Learning environments are often built for speed; keep the students moving through a bite-sized series of activities (so the philosophy goes) and they won't misbehave and get distracted.
>
> (Mycroft and Sidebottom 2017: 20)

'Busy' learning environments are the norm, with lots of energy, group work and questioning. Counter-culturally, thinking environment work, a series of applications each of which rests on ten values (or components[11]), slows the group culture down, enacting the paradox 'freedom needs boundaries' to provide a safe environment for focused thinking (Mycroft and Sidebottom 2018a). The following diagram (Figure 5.1) shows the relationship between the ten components of Kline's *Thinking Environment* (2009).

Based on similar principles, Community Philosophy acts as a pedagogy, research and cohesion tool, bridging communication across identities (such as educator and student, for example). It does not seek consensus; instead it allows for 'constructive engagement with conflict and controversy' via facilitated enquiry (Tiffany 2009: 5). With its roots in the 'Philosophy for Children' movement, Community Philosophy is effective across ages and in intergenerational settings in particular. The word 'philosophy' is arguably disruptive to an education policy which is focused on feeding a growth economy (Daley et al. 2015). Tiffany evaluated the New Earswick Community Philosophy project, which was a three-year experiment aimed at developing positive relationships across different groups of people

---

[11]Ease, appreciation, equality, information, feelings, diversity, encouragement, attention, place and incisive questions.

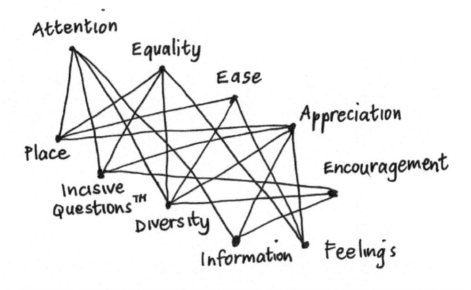

Figure 5.1 *Ten components of Kline's* Thinking Environment.

within a community. He found the approach to be not easy work but achieves, among other successful impacts, an effective 'conversational bridge' (2009: 2). In an affirmative mental health pedagogy, Community Philosophy provides a non-confrontational space to practise disagreement, enabling personal expression without the triggers of 'normal', combative discussion.

As we have seen above, restorative practice, grounded in principles of restorative justice, is gaining traction in behaviour 'management', thanks to the work of Paul Dix and others in the UK and elsewhere. With its focus on careful 'restorative' listening, in common with the *Thinking Environment*, restorative practice also slows engagement down in order to use time more effectively; little wonder, then, that a 'Slow Teaching' movement is emerging (Thom 2018). Thom's work shares with the pedagogies above the component of clear information, helping to manage anxieties by ensuring that everyone securely knows the task in hand.

Self-agency

Here's a disruptive question: why do students have to be infantilized, even if they are literally children? One of the most persistent echoes of the CLMH curation was the well-meaning, sometimes unwitting, paternalization of students by educators. Phrases such as 'my learners' and the limiting of student agency in many forms betrayed a risk-averse, protective attitude to 'vulnerability'. Clearly, educators have a duty of care with all ages of student – as human beings we are all potentially vulnerable – but there are also many honourable examples of power-sharing down the history of education,[12] which shift the responsibility of the educator along a spectrum from 'control', through the empowerment of others, to a place where risk-positive learning environments are co-constructed which allow individuals to develop agency.

Researchers for the Health and Safety Executive, the What Works Centre for Wellbeing and others have long established that one of the biggest causes of workplace stress is lack of autonomy; it's not too great a stretch to apply this to education also. There is much talk in education of 'learner resilience', a process of developing mental strength which places responsibility entirely on the student's shoulders, without conceding any quarter to the social, political and economic circumstances which they may endure. James (2015: 6) describes resilience as:

> The new means of production; this means that crisis and trauma are actually necessary, desirable phenomena – you can't bounce back without first falling.

This 'disaster capitalism' (James uses Naomi Klein's term) plays out in education via the 'tragic life story' narrative which is particularly dominant in 'second-chance' adult education. In this narrative, adults whose behavioural history have caused them to 'fail' at school (rather than schools/society failing them) are 'rescued' by adult education and 'empowered', in return for gratitude. This equates with an 'empowering others' approach which is subtly but powerfully different from creating conditions where others empower themselves.

Here, education and affirmative mental health promotion align. Berry's (2011) work for the Joseph Rowntree Foundation politicized public sector risk-aversion and Faulkner (2012), who explicitly positions herself as a mental health service user, explored the complex power relations of risk and responsibility in a mental health context. Although neither was writing directly about education, their findings offer ideas for a pedagogy which finds spaces for co-production. The educator's role is one which both provides the necessary knowledge to satisfy the curriculum and creates a 'classroom'[13] environment conducive to learning. Where control of the latter can be shared with students as equals, a healthy self-agency can take root, leading to improved academic outcomes as well as healthy behaviours – everyone wins. Co-construction of sessions, negotiated deadlines and co-facilitation of discussion are all ways of growing a shared responsibility for learning.

A sense of belonging

Malik (2017) is not the only thinker to identify how fundamental a sense of belonging is to counter the disenfranchisement from society that *could* lead to extremism. Using a talk by

---

[12]See, for example, Summerhill School: not an outdated place of privilege but a vibrant endeavour where educators work with students who experience the full range of neurodiversity, in co-operative co-productive education practices.
[13]Or wherever.

Malik as an initial stimulus, Sidebottom and Thornton (2017) took Community Philosophy enquiries out to educators around the UK, to help them move beyond the strictures of online safeguarding training and explore for themselves how they could address the requirement to embed Fundamental British Values (FBV) in their practice. Sidebottom and Thornton found educators 'hungry to think differently about the potential for democratic education' (2017: 1) yet experiencing fear, confusion and misunderstanding around their duties under the Prevent Agenda, leading to classroom spaces that no longer felt safe. Participants generated their own questions for discussion and committed to concrete professional development actions, such as doing identities and values work with groups of students.

Teaching which seeks not to homogenize but to find commonalities among difference cannot be 'done by numbers', a phrase used by Dix (2017) to challenge the orthodoxies of behaviour management practices, in favour of boundaried relationship building. It is persistent, patient work and there is no quick fix. A *Thinking Environment* culture, for example (Kline 2009), builds from initial resistance into an environment of shared responsibility, which ultimately creates a place of belonging which brings participants in from the margins, but it takes time and is painful for some: those who are used to dominating the airspace, for example, or those who take refuge in silence (Mycroft and Sidebottom 2018).

Extra curriculars

The education and popular press in the UK have been resounding with stories about 'successful' yoga and meditation interventions for several years now, even as the pressures on students and educators are ramped up by increased testing. In a 2016 meta-analysis of early research in this area, Khalsa and Butzer conclude that, despite limited sample sizes and weak research designs in some cases, there is a growing body of evidence which affirms improved health outcomes as a result of these interventions.

These are not the only 'extra-curricular' activities which build mental health pit stops into the learning environment. Academic practices such as 'tomato writing'[14] translate well to 'boot camp' environments, which may also incorporate yoga and walking breaks, water and healthy snacks (mimicking the co-working environments of freelancers) and even tongue-in-cheek 'prizes' (such as stickers) for every 100 or 1,000 words. Education – and adult education in particular – can be slow to tear down axiomatic practice; some colleges and universities demonstrate innovative practice but keep it outside of regular classroom time, needing a certain level of motivation to access.

The use of mobile digital technology is more likely to be banned in schools (and with younger people in adult education) than not; the assumption that digital will be misused is of course not inaccurate but not wholly true either. Price (2013) and many others argue

---

[14]Strictly speaking, the pomodoro approach to time management, based on the plastic tomato oven timer, which alternates intensive activity with regular breaks, ideally walking breaks https://francescocirillo.com/pages/pomodoro-technique

for a more open and educative approach to digital, on the grounds that it will help grow self-efficacy and personal ethics. As we have seen, risk-positive approaches can strengthen agency in mental well-being.

Spaces to dance (and think)

Schools kill creativity, as Ken Robinson (2014) famously said and I have co-written elsewhere (Mycroft and Sidebottom 2018) about how educational practices fail to 'let the newness in' (Rushdie 1988). It falls to the educator to create 'spaces to dance' in curricula, that allow for new thinking, innovation and creativity.

This may be through intentional practices such as structuring lessons in a *Thinking Environment* (Kline 2009, see above) or taking time out for thinking pairs or walks. It may be through digital noticeboards, such as Padlet or Pinterest, which invite new ideas, or discussions hosted outside of classroom time which amplify different voices to those who are most confident to speak face-to-face (Daley et al. 2015).

It should certainly be through the maintenance of professional networks – 'constellations of practice' (Mycroft and Sidebottom 2018) – which bring provocative, diverse thinking into the classroom space, ideas which resonate with the hidden or reserved identities of those present, not just those who are dominant. On a related, more intentional note, decolonizing curricula and educational research (Patel 2015), although ideally an organizational responsibility, will probably need to be led from the centre of the field – by educators and students acting together (see, for example, Lola Olufemi's experience as related by Qureshi 2018).

Splinters in a small box

Here is Tzviel Rofé, talking to health professionals about his own lived experience of mental ill-health, across a chasm of misunderstanding:

> It was as if I took out a splinter from a cluster of splinters that were shot from a rifle and wounded my heart. Every time that I told my story … I slowly took out the splinters from my wounded heart and put them in a small box … and then the small box full of splinters was lying in my hand; my challenging life story was processed and under control.
>
> (Rofé 2009: 473)

Opening up educational environments as places where educators, students – everyone – can be themselves in all of their mental health and other diversities is everyone's job. It is not work that can be enforced from the top (although it can be encouraged from there); at the same time, it would be naïve to think that this would be regarded as healthy progress by everyone in an organization, including those who prefer to keep silent about their own mental health challenges. Pioneering such work is not easy; as with any profound cultural change there is a process of making oneself vulnerable in the early stages in the face of resistance, challenging norms and building alliances. External networks can help with this; getting external support while driving change from within. Braidotti's (2016) identification of the two types of power – 'potestas' and 'potentia'[15] (after the Dutch philosopher Baruch Spinoza) – can be helpful here. If, as she says, a good career is one-third *potentia* to two-thirds *potestas*, perhaps then a good campaign, a culture-changing affirmative mental health campaign, can be reversed: the campaigning power of two-thirds *potentia*, with an ally at the top – an MP, a school-leader, a chief executive – with the *potestas* to drive the change home.

Summary

This chapter has offered six propositions (Table 5.1) which make up an affirmative mental health pedagogy for all ages.

Table 5.1 Six propositions

How can you make each of the six propositions work in your own context for education?		
Proposition	**Definition**	**Question**
Teaching with ease	Slowing down activity to allow students time to think	How can you slow teaching right down so that everyone can catch their breath and know that they have been heard?
Self-agency	Power-sharing, recognition of the autonomous individual	How can you create the conditions for self-agency to take root?
Sense of belonging	Recognizing commonalities among differences to reduce feeling of exclusion	How can you create a sense of belonging, which enables everyone present to take responsibility for including others?
Extra curriculars	Additional activities to promote well-being	How can you introduce non-'academic' practices which create a culture of ease?
Spaces to dance (and think)	Create areas for innovation and new thinking	How can you create spaces which let in new ideas?
Splinters in a small box	Allowing participants to reveal and discuss their own mental health challenges	How can you influence the culture of the organization, so that talking about mental health is a strengthening activity for all?

[15]*Potestas* = power as usual, political power from the top; *potentia* = campaigning power, often from the outside or ground floor.

References

Armstrong, T. (2011), *The Power of Neurodiversity: Unleashing the Advantages of Your Differently Wired Brain*, Boston: Da Capo Publishing.

Barrett, C. (2017), *Mental Health Research 2015–17*. Available online: https://mhfe.org.uk/clmh-pilots/ (accessed 12 April 2018).

Berry, L. (2011), *The Art of Living Dangerously: Risk and Regulation*, New York: Joseph Rowntree Foundation.

Bhopal, K. (2018), *White Privilege: The Myth of a Post-Racial Society*, Bristol: Policy Press.

Bhopal, K., and Rhamie, J. (2014), 'Initial Teacher Training: Understanding "Race", Diversity and Inclusion', *Race, Ethnicity and Education Special Edition: Initial Teacher Education: Developments, Dilemmas and Challenges*, 7 (3): 304–325.

Braidotti, R. (2016), *The Posthuman*, Cambridge: Polity Press.

Brown, B. (2015), *Daring Greatly*, London: Penguin.

Coffield, F., and Williamson, B. (2011), *From Exam Factories to Communities of Discovery: The Democratic Route*, London: Institute for Education.

Daley, M., Orr, K., and Petrie, J. (2015), *Further Education and the Twelve Dancing Princesses*, London: Trentham Books.

Daley, M., Orr, K., and Petrie, J. (2017), *The Principal: Power and Professionalism in Further Education*, London: Institute of Education.

Department of Health/Department for Education (DoH/DfE) (2017), *Transforming Children and Young People's Mental Health Provision: A Green Paper*, London: HM Government.

Devon, N., and Crilly, L. (2015), *Fundamentals: A Guide for Teachers, Parents and Carers on Mental Health and Self-Esteem*, London: John Blake.

Dix, P. (2017), *When the Adults Change, Everything Changes: Seismic Shifts in School Behaviour*, Carmarthen: Independent Thinking Press.

Dweck, C. (2012), *Mindset: How You Can Fulfil Your Potential*, London: Robinson.

Dweck, C. (2017), *Mindset – Updated Version: Changing the Way You Think to Fulfil Your Potential*, London: Penguin.

Education Support Partnership (2017), *Health Survey 2017: The Mental Health and Wellbeing of Education Professionals*. Available online: https://www.educationsupportpartnership.org.uk/resources/research-reports/2017-health-survey"uk/resources/research-reports/2017-health-survey (accessed 20 May 2018).

Elliot, V., Baird, J.-A., Hopfenbeck, T., Ingram, J., Thompson, I., Usher, N., Zantout, M., with Richardson, J., and Coleman, R. (2016), *A Marked Improvement? Review of the Evidence on Written Marking*, Oxford: Education Endowment Foundation.

Faulkner, A. (2012), *The Right to Take Risks: Service Users' Views of Risk in Adult Social Care*, York: Joseph Rowntree Foundation.

Gilbert, S., and Gubar, S. (2000), *The Madwoman in the Attic: The Woman Writer and the Nineteenth-Century Literary Imagination*, Yale: Yale University Press.

Greet, P. (2017), 'Writer as Perv: Bricolage, Bowerbirding, Observation', *New Writing*, 14 (2): 184–195.

Hammersley, M. (2001), 'Some Questions About Evidence-Based Practice in Education', paper presented at the symposium on *Evidence-based Practice in Education* at the Annual

Conference of the British Educational Research Association, University of Leeds, England, 13–15 September.

Hastrup, Kirsten (1990), 'The Ethnographic Present: A Reinvention', *Cultural Anthropology*, 5 (1): 45–61.

hooks, b. (1994), *Teaching to Transgress*, New York: Routledge.

Hopkins, B. (2004), *Just Schools: A Whole-School Approach to Restorative Justice*, London: Jessica Kingsley Publications.

Iredale, A. (2018), *Teacher Education in Lifelong Learning: Developing Professionalism as a Democratic Endeavour*, London: Palgrave Macmillan.

James, R. (2015), *Resilience and Melancholy: Pop Music, Feminism and Neo-Liberalism*, Alresford: Zero Books.

Jones, G. (2016), *Evidence Based Practice: A Handbook for Teachers and School Leaders*, 26 February. Available online: http://evidencebasededucationalleadership.blogspot.com/ (accessed 12 April 2018).

Khalsa, S.B.S., and Butzer, B. (2016), 'Yoga in School Settings: A Research Review', *Annals of the New York Academy of Sciences Special Edition: Advances in Meditation Research*, 1371 (1): 45–55.

Klein, N. (2007), *The Shock Doctrine: The Rise of Disaster Capitalism*, London: Penguin.

Kline, N. (2009), *More Time to Think*, Burley-in-Wharfedale: Fisher King.

Lemov, D. (2010), *Teach Like a Champion: 49 Techniques that put Students on the Path to College*, New Jersey: Jossey Bass.

Malik, K. (2017), *From Fatwa to Jihad: How the World Changed from the Satanic Verses to Charlie Hebdo*, London: Atlantic Books.

Mirsky, L. (2007), 'SaferSanerSchools: Transforming School Cultures with Restorative Practices', *Reclaiming Children and Youth*, 16 (2): 5–12.

Mycroft, L., and Sidebottom, K. (2017), 'Using Thinking Environments for Emancipatory Coaching Practice', *Working Papers from CollectiveEd: The Hub for Mentoring and Coaching*, Leeds: Leeds Beckett University.

Mycroft, L., and Sidebottom, K. (2018), 'Constellations of Practice', in R. Smith and P. Bennett (eds), *Identity and Resistance in Further Education*, 171–180, London: Routledge.

Mycroft, L., and Weatherby, J. (2014), *Social Media Spaces*. Available online: https://practitionerledactionresearch2014.wordpress.com/multimodal-research-reports/research-reports/using-technology/ (accessed 25 April 2018).

Mycroft, L., and Weatherby, J. (2017), 'Social Purpose Leadership: A New Hope', in M. Daley, K. Orr and J. Petrie (eds), *The Principal: Power and Professionalism in Further Education*, London: Trentham Books.

National Education Union (2018), *Edu-facts: Teacher Recruitment and Retention*. Available online: https://www.teachers.org.uk/edufacts/teacher-recruitment-and-retention (accessed 21 April 2018).

Patel, L. (2015), *Decolonizing Educational Research: From Ownership to Answerability*, London: Routledge.

Perkins, R., and Slade, M. (2012), 'Recovery in England: Transforming Statutory Services?', *International Review of Psychiatry*, 24: 29–39.

Price, D. (2013), *Open: How We'll Work, Live and Learn in the Future*, London: Crux Publishing.

Qureshi, S. (2018), 'Why Are Women of Colour Still So Underrepresented in Academia?', *Media Diversified*, 17 January. Available online: https://mediadiversified.org/2018/01/17/why-are-women-of-colour-still-so-underrepresented-in-academia/ (accessed 12 May 2018).

Robinson, K. (2014), 'Do Schools Kill Creativity?', TED Talk Online. Available online: https://www.ted.com/talks/ken_robinson_says_schools_kill_creativity/transcript?language=en (accessed 24 May 2018).

Rofe, T. (2009), 'Metaphorical Stories for Education About Mental Health Challenges and Stigma', *Schizophrenia Bulletin*, 35 (3): 473–475.

Reay, D. (2017), *Miseducation: Inequality, Education and the Working Classes*, Bristol: Policy Press.

Rushdie, S. (1988), *The Satanic Verses: A Novel*, New York: Random House.

Sidebottom, K., and Thornton, K. (2017), 'Prevent as an Opportunity to Educate Out Hate', *FE News*, 15 March. Available online: https://www.fenews.co.uk/featured-article/13472-prevent-as-an-opportunity-to-educate-out-hate (accessed 20 April 2018).

Teachwire and Leeds Beckett University (2018), *Investigation into Teachers' Mental Health*. Available online: https://www.teachwire.net/news/pupil-progress-is-being-held-back-by-teachers-poor-mental-health"eld-back-by-teachers-poor-mental-health (accessed 21 May 2018).

Thom, J. (2018), *Slow Teaching: On Finding Calm, Clarity and Impact in the Classroom*, Melton: John Catt Educational.

Thorley, C. (2017), *Not By Degrees: Improving Student Mental Health in the UK's Universities*, London: IPPR.

Tiffany, G.A. (2009), *Community Philosophy: A Project Report*, New York: Joseph Rowntree Foundation (JRF).

Tingle, J. (2017), 'How the NHS Is Failing Patients with Mental Health Problems', *British Journal of Nursing*, 27 (0): 510–511.

Warner, D. (1998), *Nothing About Us without Us: Developing Innovative Technologies for, by and with Disabled Persons*, California: Healthwrights.

Williams, B. (2002), *Truth and Truthfulness: An Essay in Genealogy*, Princeton: Princeton University Press.

Wilson, R. (2014), *Anti-Hero: The Hidden Revolution in Leadership and Change*, London: OSCA.

6 Using Research-Informed Teaching to Support Behaviour Management in FE

DAVID POWELL

Introduction: research as a basis for teaching

> The justification for research as a basis for ... teaching is the perspective to be gained from the hill of inquiry over the plain of knowledge.
> **STENHOUSE 1979: 9**

This chapter seeks to move beyond the practical advice offered in the 'instrumental "how-to" category' (Wallace 2014: 348) of books and considers how research on behaviour management undertaken in further education (FE) and schools might offer insights into this complex issue, inform practice and suggest new areas for research. Teachers need practical advice on behaviour management, although they need to know the basis for the 'how-to' advice. Teachers' professional learning is the 'interplay' between the 'practical wisdom' derived from teaching and the 'public knowledge' of research about teaching (Boyd 2014: 54). However, few authors writing about behaviour management in FE discuss in any detail the research on it (for instance, Vizard 2012).

> Without data, you are just another person with an opinion.
> **(SCHLEICHER QUOTED BY WILBY 2013: N.P.)**

Schleicher's assertion is that we need research to understand what does and does not work if we are to improve students' learning and achievement. Practical 'how-to' guides on managing behaviour making no reference to the research behind its claims are just one person's practical wisdom. It may be very good advice, although we need research evidence to judge the quality of the advice. Based on research, Coe et al. (2014: 3) identify six factors that underpin what they call great teaching; they rank classroom climate and classroom management third and fourth in the list and state they have 'moderate evidence of impact on student outcomes'. But what is research?

Stenhouse (1981: 113) defined research as 'systematic and sustained inquiry, planned and self-critical, which is subjected to public criticism and to empirical tests where these are appropriate'. Within education, there are two applications of research for teaching:

teaching-led research and research-led teaching. Teaching-led research involves a teacher (or team) researching an aspect of their practice to better understand it or improve it. They could use action research, for instance, to do this. Second, research-led teaching is when a teacher uses their own research, or others, to inform, plan and design their teaching. However, Nosek, an American professor, warns teachers to be careful before adopting the latest research findings into their practice as 'education … is a field particularly susceptible to research problems' (Parr 2018: 42). This is not to say that all research should be ignored. We need to understand the strengths and weaknesses of its research design and evaluate its claims based on this, which requires 'research literacy' (Bennett 2015: n.p). At the same time, teachers need to be mindful that 'no single study is definitive, no matter how big, or how extensive. Each study is part of an accumulating body of evidence' (Parr 2018: 42).

An overview of research on behaviour management in further education (FE)

Ain't Misbehavin' (Mitchell et al. 1998) appears to be the first example of research into disruptive behaviour in FE. Binner's (2011) doctorate based on a case study of disruptive behaviour at an English FE college was next. Then NIACE (2012) undertook research on unemployed adults' disruptive behaviour on training courses, perhaps the only research on adults' disruptive behaviour in FE. More recent published research includes journal articles (Lebor 2013a and b; Wallace 2014, for example), reports (Parry and Taubman 2013) and books (Lebor 2017). Table 6.1 a and b provides a summary of this research.

UCU's Whole College Behaviour Management study: a case study

The University and College Union (UCU), the largest trade union in England for FE, commissioned this study. The research was prompted by union members asking for advice and help about student behaviour at a time when 'more students with behavioural issues' were enrolling at colleges and funding pressures meant that recruitment, retention and achievement had even greater importance (Parry and Taubman 2013: 3). The findings of this study are rarely cited in literature or discussed. For example, Lebor (2017) cites the report but focuses his discussion on a short quotation from page two of the report. Based on the analysis of 400 online surveys completed by UCU members, reviews of thirty colleges' behaviour management policies, and interviews with managers, support staff, teachers and students at eight colleges, this is the largest study of behaviour management in FE and its findings are illuminating and deserve a wider audience.

There are six key findings:

1 Its literature review recognizes that most of the research has been done on disruptive behaviour in schools, adding 'a great deal of this could be transferable to the FE sector if it were contextualised' (Parry and Taubman 2013: 57).

Table 6.1(a) Initial analysis of research undertaken on disruptive behaviour in FE

Date	Author and their positionality	Focus of the study	Methodology*	Methods	Participants	Sites
1998	Mitchell et al. (independent consultants)	To develop 'practical strategies.... and policy models' (1998: 21)	Action research	Self-assessment exercise; action plan; supported training; feedback; college materials	Teachers	8 colleges
2011	Binner (FE-based teacher)	To study what shapes student's behaviour and identify strategies to reduce disruptive behaviour	Case study/ action research	Interviews; card sorting exercise; documentary evidence	20 students	1 college in Yorkshire
2012	NIACE (DBIS funded research)	To support behaviour management within skills provision for adults	Action research	Interviews	Senior managers, operations managers, tutors, curriculum managers	18 colleges
2013	Parry and Taubman (UCU sponsored research)	To develop 'a model whole college behaviour policy.... [for] to the FE sector and to UCU FE branches and members' (UCU 2013: 3)	Action research	Online survey; interviews; documentary evidence	400 UCU members participated in the online survey. Managers, teachers, support staff, security staff and students from 8 colleges	8 colleges
2013a	Lebor (FE-based teacher educator)	To support trainee teachers to manage disruptive behaviour	Multiple case studies	Field notes	2 trainee teachers	1 college
2013b	Lebor (FE-based teacher educator)	Developing strategies to support trainee teachers to deal with disruptive behaviour	Self-study	'Observation of classrooms and reflective practice' (Lebor 2018, pers. comm)	1 teacher educator	1 college

*Italics indicate methodology the researchers seem to have adopted. In Lebor's research, this has been checked with the author directly.

Table 6.1(b)

Year	Author	Aim	Methodology	Methods	Sample	Setting
2014	Wallace	To identify disruptive behaviour and its causes and how teachers dealt with it. To identify any changes required in ITE and CPD to support teachers	*Multiple case studies*	Focus groups; lesson observations	203 teachers	3 colleges
2014	Lebor (FE-based teacher educator)	To identify teachers' experience of disruptive behaviours and how they dealt with it.	*Multiple case studies*	Individual interviews	30 teachers	'A variety of educational institutions' (2014: 14)
2015a	Lebor (FE-based teacher educator)	To share strategies for students who are resistant to learning and assessment	*'Auto-ethnographic case study'*	Field notes	1 researcher and 1 student	1 college
2015b	Lebor (FE-based teacher educator)	To listen to students about their disruptive behaviour and use this to inform staff development for teachers	*Action research*	Survey	'around 60 students and 6 tutors'	'different colleges'
2016	Lebor (FE-based teacher educator)	To identify 'how might managers in the lifelong learning sector support tutors in dealing with' disruptive behaviour (2016: 568).	*'Qualitative practitioner research' (2016: 568).*	Survey for managers; survey for teachers; two focus groups with managers; interview with manager	25 managers and 34 teachers	'different... colleges in Yorkshire' (2016: 572).
2017	Lebor (FE-based teacher educator)	To identify how teacher educators prepare trainees for disruptive classes and what trainees said about their ITE and how it was preparing them to deal with classroom disruption	*'Qualitative research' (2017: 171)*	Survey of teacher educators; focus groups and interviews with teacher educators; questionnaires; focus groups with trainees	200 Trainees and 35 teacher educators	'two dozen teacher education departments' (2017: 170)

2 FE 'needs to develop its own behaviour management policies and strategies' (Parry and Taubman 2013).

3 The sector 'needs to learn from colleges who have developed whole college proactive behaviour policies' (Parry and Taubman 2013). What the report does not say is that one way the sector could learn from what seems to be effective practice is by researching it and determining its transferability to other educational sites and settings.

4 At an organizational level, it points out that colleges are different from schools in two ways. They are larger and their students represent 'a much more diverse student body including both young people and adults, many of who study on a part time basis' (Parry and Taubman 2013: 18). Learning often takes place at several different sites, where departmentalism may have a greater influence on the 'sayings, doings, and relatings' (Kemmis et al. 2014a: 31) of staff and student practices than the college.

5 UCU members identified twenty-seven different forms of problematic behaviour, and these might be categorized as 'minor disruption'; 'non-participation'; 'very serious risks' (Parry and Taubman 2013: 24). While UCU does not classify the behaviours, I have attempted this. Table 6.2 lists the top ten and the bottom five disruptive behaviours and their proposed category.

Table 6.2 The top 10 and bottom 5 disruptive behaviours identified in study

Rank	Behaviour	Proposed classification of behaviour	Responses	Percentage
1	Distracting others	Minor disruption	313	79.8
2	Poor attendance	Non-participation	305	77.8
3	Low-level disruption	Minor disruption	262	66.8
4	Attention seeking	Minor disruption	253	64.5
5	Swearing	Minor disruption	243	62
6	Inattention	Non-participation	235	59.9
7	Uncooperativeness	Minor disruption	231	58.9
8	Absence	Non-participation	230	58.7
9	Handing in work late	Non-participation	225	57.4
10	Not undertaking assignments	Non-participation	207	52.8
23	Stealing	Very serious risks	44	11.2
24	Alcohol abuse	Very serious risks	34	8.7
25	Racial abuse	Very serious risks	31	7.9
26	Physical abuse	Very serious risks	29	7.4
27	Extortion	Very serious risks	4	1
(number of responses = 400)				
(Adapted from Parry and Taubman 2013: 35)				

What seems to be missing from this list? Fighting is ranked 16th; drug taking is ranked 20th, and there is no mention of the use of mobile phones.[1]

6 Participants suggested nine factors that shaped students' behaviour:

- the college's rules and procedures and how they were developed, interpreted and implemented;
- the use of rewards and sanctions by staff and students' responses to it;
- the quality of inductions for new staff, especially for part-time hourly paid staff;
- the extent to which teachers and support staff worked as a team to address disruptive behaviour and support disruptive students;
- the quality and consistency of student inductions, for example, what happens when students enrol late onto a programme;
- increased class sizes meant there is less time for 1:1 support;
- teaching spaces used;
- a student's disposition to learning;
- socio-economic factors.[2]

What is the value of the UCU research? First, it is a resource for professional conversations about disruptive behaviour. Staff Development might use the list when they plan continuous professional development for their staff. Note that almost 40 per cent of the UCU members had not received any training to support them when dealing with disruptive behaviour and almost 45 per cent of those that had completed initial teacher education programmes said it had not been covered within their award (Parry and Taubman 2013: 36). Second, it contributes to 'a map' (Petrie 2015: 7) of what is known about behaviour management in FE.

Mapping FE-based research and identifying 'the blank spaces on the map'

Research about FE-based teachers' practice and students' disruptive behaviour helps us better understand this complex issue; it can act as a map (Figure 6.1) and guide for teachers seeking to 'find their way around that [particular] swamp of practice' (Berry 2008: 31). For instance, NIACE's research illuminates what is known about adults' disruptive behaviour:

---

[1] See Wallace's study (2014) which reported that students disrupted learning by using mobile phones in 132 of 183 observed classes.
[2] Wallace (2014) and Binner (2011) studies both discussed factors shaping student behaviour and identified similar points. Wallace provides two further insights that are noteworthy. First, 'teacher attitudes and attributes rather than skills and strategies' (2014: 357) seemed to impact positively on behaviour; Wallace suggests a teacher's 'cheerfulness' (2014) was seen as an important factor in student engagement. Second, some students were disengaged because they had 'learned attitudes towards education and training' (2014).

The incidence of challenging behaviour increases after learners stop being on their best behaviour at about two days into the provision … incidents reach a peak by the second week and … reduce as learners become more and more accustomed to routines of the learning environment and expectations of tutors and other learners … A tutor, using negotiated ground rules, said that on peak days she has to refer learners to the ground rules about five times a day. (NIACE 2012:14)

Where are the 'blank spaces' on this map? It seems only the qualitative area has begun to be 'mapped' so far (Berry 2008: 31). This needs to be addressed; the best people to 'fill in the blank spaces on the map' are teachers and teacher educators. One of these 'spaces' is the use of quantitative research methodologies to evaluate the effectiveness of strategies in FE, although we have to turn to research done in schools in the United States for examples of how to do it.

Marzano, Marzano and Pickering's use of effect sizes to identify the most effective strategies for managing behaviour: a case study

This research is rarely cited by authors writing about behaviour management in FE; only Petty (2006) and Lebor (2017) mention it, the latter discussing the strategy of rules and procedures rather than referring to their effect size. This research falls into the category Parry and Taubman (2013: 57) described as 'transferable to the FE sector if it were contextualised'.

	Types of study		
Participants	Qualitative studies	Qualitative and quantitative studies	Quantitative studies
Students	Binner (2011)		
Support staff			
Students and teachers	Lebor (2015b)		
Students, teachers, support staff, security staff, and managers		Parry and Taubman (2013)	
Trainee teachers	Lebor (2013a)		
Trainee teachers and teacher educators	Lebor (2017)		
Teacher educators	Lebor (2013b)		
Teachers	Mitchell et al. (1998) Lebor (2014) Lebor (2015a)	Wallace (2014)	
Teachers and managers	NIACE (2012) Lebor (2016)		
Managers			
Security staff			

Terra incognita

Figure 6.1 *A provisional 'map' of the FE-based research on behaviour management along the lines of an ordnance survey map, with the horizontal grid lines, in this instance, reflecting the methodology and the vertical lines the study's focus.*

While reading this section ask yourself this question: how much of the practical 'how-to' guide advice seems to be based on this research? Make a note of anything you notice.

Marzano et al. (2003) used quantitative research techniques to synthesize over 100 existing pieces of research to create a larger data set for meta-analysis and from this draw generalizable conclusions about classroom management. They combined ten studies on the effective use of rules and procedures in classes. This increased the sample from an average of just over sixty per study, which quantitative researchers would have less statistical confidence in, to a sample of 636.[3] From this, they identified four factors that shape teachers' classroom management,[4] and these are presented in rank order in Table 6.3.

What does the table mean? The first column is the factor shaping classroom management. The second tells us the number of studies included in the calculation, the third the number of students involved in those studies. This is important information for teachers and researchers as the number of the studies and students can increase our confidence in the effect size, which is column four. The effect size is a calculation that tells us what impact a teacher effectively employing the 'factor' has compared with a teacher who does not use it (or uses it ineffectively); the fifth column translates the effect size into a percentile reduction.

How do we read this research? The meta-analysis of teachers' mental set, which is a combination of what is called teacher 'withitness', their ability to quickly and accurately identify and address problem behaviour, or potentially problem behaviour, and 'emotional objectivity', is based on five studies that involved 502 students. The effect size was −1.294 and using a table to convert effect size to percentile decrease (see Marzano et al. 2003: 119) it is equivalent to a 40 percentile decrease in disruption. They emphasize this is not to say there is no disruption. It means that if the average number of disruptions in a class where

Table 6.3 *The effectiveness of four factors that shape teachers' classroom management*

Factor	Number of studies	Number of students	Average effect size	Percentile decrease in disruptions
Mental set	5	502	−1.294	40
Disciplinary interventions	68	3,322	−0.909	32
Teacher–student relationships	4	1,110	−0.869	31
Rules and procedures	10	626	−0.763	28
Note: All effect sizes are significant at the 0.05 level. Teachers used only one factor for the intervention and measured its impact. (adapted from Marzano, Marzano and Pickering 2003: 8)				

[3]See Gorard 2001 for a discussion on sample sizes in quantitative research.
[4]It is important to be aware the meta-analysis combined different 'grades' of school. This does not mean we should disregard it. Instead, we might need to adapt the disciplinary interventions to our context and research their impact on our students' behaviour.

the factor is not being employed is twenty on any given day then a teacher who effectively employs mental set will reduce disruptions, on average, to twelve a day. Importantly, mental set is learnable and most teachers' classroom management skills 'could be significantly improved ... by the simple intervention of providing them with a manual and two half-day workshops' (Marzano et al. 2003: 11). The research claims that a teacher who can learn these behaviours and effectively use them is likely to have fewer disruptions because of this and their students' learning and achievement should be better. Each of the four factors is now considered in turn.

Teachers' mental set 'consistently differentiates' those who effectively manage behaviour from those who are less effective (Marzano et al. 2003: 5). Of the two elements of mental set, it is 'withitness' that has the higher average effect size and can reduce disruption by 42 per cent. However, this calculation is based on a small number of studies – three – and a sample of 426 students and, likely, would be lower if there had been more studies warns Marzano. Nevertheless, Hattie (2012: 70) concurs that teachers need 'withitness' skills if they are to effectively manage their classroom. Brophy suggested teachers stay 'with it' by continuously scanning the classroom, even when working with small groups or individuals. Where teachers stand in their classrooms can help the scanning required for spotting the beginnings of disruptive behaviour and a whole-class reminder about focusing on their work can be used if the teacher is unsure who is behind a disruption (Hattie 2012).

However, being 'with it' is not 'our typical frame of mind' (Hattie 2012: 65) as teachers are not used to or skilled in 'the discipline of noticing' (Mason 2002), which is at the heart of it. Teaching, learning and assessment are essentially complex, 'messy, elusive ... [and] unpredictable' (Coffield 2014: 113) and might appear as a 'confusing' mess (Schön 1983: 42) to a new teacher. One way they suggest you might gain a better appreciation of 'withitness' is by watching another teacher who is well known for skilfully managing disruptive learners teach their group. The advent of technology like IRIS Connect © allows teachers to watch a class without being intrusive. Marzano et al. (2003) provide advice on how to develop your ability to react to disruption and forecast it too.

The second dimension to a teacher's mental set is their 'emotional objectivity', which enables them to address disruptive behaviour in an emotionally detached way. How a teacher views their students and their disruptive behaviour determines their 'emotional objectivity'. Teachers who personalize the disruption may react in ways that can damage the teacher–student relationship. Not being objective is one of the behaviours students see as inappropriate for teachers. Therefore, while it may be initially difficult to maintain 'emotional objectivity', it is important for teachers to be aware of it and practise it. One way they might do this is by undertaking a self-study into their own practice and recording how they feel in their classes and noticing the impact of their behaviour on their students' behaviours. Self-study is a methodology for researching our teaching and I explore it later in this chapter.

Marzano, Marzano and Pickering identified five categories of disciplinary intervention that seemed to work. They are presented in Table 6.4.

Table 6.4 Effect sizes for disciplinary interventions

Intervention	Number of studies	Number of students	Average effect size	Percentile decrease in disruptions
Teacher reaction	25	1191	−0.997	34
Group contingency	13	413	−0.981	34
Tangible recognition	20	672	−0.823	29
Direct cost	7	243	−0.569	21
Home contingency	3	169	−0.555	21
(adapted from Marzano, Marzano and Pickering 2003: 30)				

Teacher reaction is how teachers communicate – verbally and non-verbally – to students that their behaviour is acceptable or unacceptable. Group contingency puts students into groups and applies the principle of collective responsibility by requiring group members to meet an acceptable level of stated behaviour. Tangible recognition is a reward system in which teachers 'reward' good behaviour (2003: 29) and any instances of poor behaviour result in rewards being withdrawn. Direct cost involves a specific consequence for certain types of disruptive behaviour. Home contingency extends the rules and procedures into a student's home, and behaviour is monitored by parents/guardians/carers and reported back to the teacher.

Teacher–student relationships are 'the keystone' of classroom management (2003: 41) and can reduce disruption by 31 per cent. However, the research warns that this calculation is based on only four studies and is 'much larger' (2003) than is normally found in social sciences. They suggest that if more studies were carried out then the average effect size would be lower. They complement their meta-analysis of the teacher–student relationship with what they describe as 'perceptual evidence' (2003: 41) from other studies. For instance, a study of sixty-eight high school students asked what caused the disruption in classrooms; fifty-seven of them stated that fewer behavioural problems would have happened if there had been a better teacher–student relationship. One explanation given for this is that teachers are unable to establish democratic classrooms and instead operate classrooms based on a 'we-they' power-based relationship. This seems to be an example of the practice architectures of the school/college, specifically the social-political arrangements, in terms of power, shaping the practices of teachers' teaching and thus students' learning (Kemmis et al. 2014a: 38).

Marzano, Marzano and Pickering cite research conducted in the Netherlands by Wubbels's team (1999) into the ideal student–teacher relationship. This research identified two dimensions – cooperation and dominance – which interact and create a teacher–student relationship. The relationship is dynamic and can adjust over time as a result of the teacher shifting their position in terms of cooperation and dominance. High dominance teachers are controlling in their approach and overly focused on what needs to be done, with little regard for the students and their interests. High submission is too student-centred and tends to defer to what the students want to do rather than what they need to do. Teachers adopting a high cooperation approach want to be liked by the students and so are too student-focused and democratic. They listen to students or consult them too much and do not challenge them enough. High opposition is at the other end of the continuum and sees students as 'the enemy' (Petty 2006: 7). The teacher's will controls the classroom; they are in charge. The research suggests that the optimal relationship is 'moderate to high dominance … and moderate to high cooperation' (Marzano et al. 2003: 43). Many new teachers, in an attempt to be liked, are overly cooperative and often submissive (unless they have considerable leadership experience). However, as they become more experienced, normally after '6 to 10 years' of teaching, they become confident and 'competent' at being dominant and 'less cooperative' (Marzano et al. 2003: 44). Unfortunately, this less cooperative approach damages the student–teacher relationship. Petty (2006) usefully suggests how to apply this piece of research into FE-based teaching.

Teaching behaviours that sustain good teacher–student relationships identified by Wubbels's team's research include:

- Effective teaching
- Being 'friendly, helpful, and congenial'
- Empathetic
- Good listener
- Effective communicators
- 'Not gloomy' (links to 'cheerfulness' mentioned by Wallace 2014)
- Even tempered
- Have high expectations
- Maintain control of their classroom
- Create an environment in which learners take responsibility for their own learning.

(Marzano et al. 2003: 44)

What do students say about student–teacher relationships? Research undertaken with 712 school pupils suggested almost 60 per cent of them preferred teachers adopting a 'confronting/contracting' style (Marzano et al. 2003), attending to disciplinary problems that arise in a flexible way. They also cite Brophy's research that suggests the most effective teachers and managers use highly differentiated behaviour management strategies that consider individual students' personal circumstances. Less effective teachers tended to stick to the same strategy irrespective of the student.

Students' and their parents' views on how schools and colleges should deal with disruptive behaviour is discussed too. It cites research into what 'college students' considered to be 'inappropriate' behaviour by their teachers (Marzano et al. 2003: 32) that makes interesting reading. Based on a sample of 254 students, some of the inappropriate behaviours included:

a Missing classes;

b Being late;

c Ending classes early;

d Being unprepared for classes and disorganized;

e Late returning their work;

f Being sarcastic or publicly criticizing a student;

g Unfair rules;

h Not answering students' questions;

i Being unfair or inconsistent;

If students perceive their teachers as hard-working, fair and consistent, they are more likely to comply with attempts to manage their behaviour. Other research cited by Marzano et al. (2003) suggested that students' behaviour deteriorated as they move through school. They explain this is as a result of maturation, their disposition towards learning and the curriculum being taught.[5]

Rules and procedures are the architectures that create the classroom climate. There are two types: school/college-level and class-level, which are often called ground rules. When effectively employed they can reduce disruptions by 28 per cent. Rules and procedures need to be carefully explained to students and teachers should involve their groups when writing them (2003: 17). How many rules should you have? This research suggests no more than seven rules and procedures for students on FE equivalent courses. How many have your students got? Dix (2017: 162) often asks head teachers he is working with how many of the rules your students know and can tell you. That would be a good question to ask your students; a piece of research perhaps?

And teachers had 'firmly established management routines by the sixth day' of the academic year (2017: 93). How often is this the case in your school/college? What shapes this happening in your college/institution? Research suggests the most effective teachers spent time before the start of the academic year planning for classroom management. When the classes started they spent more time than other teachers on establishing the ground rules and procedures for the class, ensuring their students accepted them, and implementing them until keeping the rules was routine behaviour. The research highlighted the need for rules and procedures for group work too. These included setting up the task; explaining how the group should operate; stating expected activities and behaviour during the task;

---

[5]See Wallace 2014.

emphasizing who in the group can communicate with the teacher; checking with the group before the task starts what they are going to do.

A final point from this research: where you teach and how it is led does shape your management of learning and behaviour, although it argues teachers can still effectively manage behaviour in poorly led colleges or institutions. However, the most impactful classroom management is a product of effective teacher practice which is sustained by effective leadership and management of the college (Marzano et al. 2003: 3).

Researching 'the blank spaces' on the FE behaviour management 'research map'

Berry (2008: 31) states research on teaching requires researchers to enter 'the swamp of practice'; 'a complex and messy terrain, often difficult to describe [and map]'. However, she does not say it is impossible. Cotton undertook research that 'estimated … only about half of all classroom time is used for instruction, and disciplinary problems occupy most of the other half' (Marzano et al. 2003: 27). Has anyone in FE in England analysed their classes in the same way? Why would you? How would you undertake such a study? Would you film it? Note that there are important ethical considerations related to filming classes, although these can be overcome by following the British Educational Research Association's (2018) guidelines. By filming your class would you better understand your classroom in terms of your 'sayings, doings, and relatings' and your students' 'sayings, doings, and relatings' (Kemmis et al. 2014a: 31)?

Three types of research useful for a teacher-researcher are action research, self-study and supported experiments. Kemmis et al. (2014b: 4) describe action research as 'a practice-changing practice' that 'aims to change practices, people's understanding of their practices, and the conditions under which they practice' (2014b: 59). Self-study is 'a methodology for studying professional practice settings' (Pinnegar 1998 cited by Laboskey 2008: 252), with the aim of improving practice. Supported experiments (Petty 2018) are team-based and might be regarded as a form of action research. They require teams to identify the most important area of improvement in their practice, request training to support it and then practise and experiment with the 'new teaching approach … and gradually adapting it until it works. These experiments are done for the team and they are supported by the team. Once you have found a way of making a strategy work you tell your team about it and they adopt it' (Petty 2018: n.p.).

What types of research might be undertaken using these methodologies? Teachers might use self-study to improve their own 'withitness' by filming one (or more) of their own classes and reviewing it with a colleague. Supported experiments might be used to study the impact of introducing a new disciplinary intervention. An action research study might look at the introduction of ground rules at the start of the year and the impact on student behaviour over the first two weeks of term and then again later in the year. Essentially, I am suggesting that some of the earlier studies done by Marzano and others are replicated in FE and published in journals like *Teaching in Lifelong Learning*, an FE-focused journal aimed at informing and improving practice. Such an approach will help FE create a more comprehensive knowledge base of behaviour management for the sector, although for some 'it is the extent to which [the research] contributes to history – to changing, for the better, the world [of education for its teachers and learners]' (Kemmis et al. 2014b: 27) that is even more important.

Who can support your research aspirations? Ask for financial support from your college/institution first; this could help you enrol on a postgraduate degree. Also, the Education and Training Foundation's Practitioner Research programme supports new researchers implement their research ideas.

Towards some conclusions

This chapter makes three points. First, teachers' professional learning requires them to engage with more than the 'how to' guides if they are to effectively manage students' behaviour; their teaching needs to be research-informed. Second, there is a limited but growing research literature on and relevant to behaviour management in FE, although some of it is not well known and rarely cited. Teachers need to know what research is available for them to read and then use it in their practice. Third, there seem to be significant 'blank spaces on the map' of FE-based research into behaviour management. This needs to be addressed and teachers have a choice of research methodologies to choose from if they want to take up this challenge, learn from it and in the process make their FE college or institution a better place to study and work at.

Activities

Two concluding questions for you:

1   How might you apply what you have learned from reading this chapter in your own teaching and research practice?
2   What support might you need to apply what you have learned? Who might help you?

Acknowledgement

I would like to thank Geoff Petty for his correspondence with me during the writing of this chapter and the materials he shared with me.

References

Bennett, T. (2015), 'Thoughts on the Carter Review: The Unenforceable Sec's Machine', *TES*. Available online: https://www.tes.com/news/blog/thoughts-carter-review-unenforceable-secs-machine (accessed 4 June 2018).

Berry, A. (2008), *Tensions in Teaching About Teaching: Understanding Practice as a Teacher Educator*, Dordrecht: Springer.

Binner, C. (2011), *Who Me? What Did I Do? A Case Study to Explore Learner Perceptions of Reasons for Persistent Disruptive Behaviour and the Possible Outcome of This in Level Two Classes in a College of Further Education*, Doctoral thesis, University of Huddersfield. Available online: http://eprints.hud.ac.uk/12141/ (accessed 27 March 2018).

Boyd, P. (2014), 'Using Modelling to Improve the Coherence of Initial Teacher Education', in P. Boyd, A. Szplit and Z. Zbróg (eds), *Teacher Educators and Teachers as Learners: International Perspectives*, 51–74, Krakow: Libron.

British Educational Research Association (2018), *Ethical Guidelines for Educational Research*, 4th edn, London: BERA.

Coe, R., Aloisi, C., Higgins, S., and Elliot Major, L. (2014), *What Makes Great Teaching? Review of the Underpinning Research*, Durham: Durham University, Sutton Trust.

Coffield, F. (2014), 'Whip Me with Carrots: The Role of Motivation in Education and Training', in F. Coffield, with C. Costa, W. Müller and J. Webber (eds), *Beyond Bulimic Learning: Improving Teaching in Further Education*, 99–116, London: IOE Press.

Dix, P. (2017), *When the Adults Change Everything Changes: Seismic Shifts in School Behaviour*, Carmarthen: Independent Thinking Press.

Gorard, S. (2001), *Quantitative Methods in Educational Research*, London: Continuum.

Hattie, J. (2012), *Visible Learning for Teachers: Maximising Impact for Learning*, Abingdon: Routledge.

Kemmis, S., Wilkinson, J., Edwards-Groves, C., Hardy, I., Grootenboer, P., and Bristol, L. (2014a), *Changing Practices, Changing Education*, London: Springer.

Kemmis, S., McTaggart, R., and Nixon, R. (2014b), *The Action Research Planner: Doing Critical Participatory Action Research*, Dordrecht: Springer.

Laboskey, V.K. (2008), 'The Fragile Strengths of Self-Study', in P. Aubusson and S. Schuck (eds), *Teacher Learning and Development: The Mirror Maze*, 251–262, Dordrecht: Springer.

Lebor, M. (2013a), 'Class Wars: Initial Steps into the Fray', *Teaching in Lifelong Learning: A Journal to Inform and Improve Practice*, 4 (2): 14–23.

Lebor, M. (2013b), 'War and Peace in the Classroom: Moments of Reprieve: A Strategy for Reflecting on Improving Classroom Behaviour', *Teaching in Lifelong Learning: A Journal to Inform and Improve Practice*, 5 (1): 21–31.

Lebor, M. (2014), 'War Stories: How Experienced Teachers Said They Responded to Disruptive Students in the Lifelong Learning Sector', *Teaching in Lifelong Learning: A Journal to Inform and Improve Practice*, 5 (2): 12–21.

Lebor, M. (2015a), 'The Fear of Being Assessed', *Teaching in Lifelong Learning: A Journal to Inform and Improve Practice*, 6 (2): 5–15.

Lebor, M. (2015b), 'What Disruptive Students Said They Wanted from Their Classes', *Teaching in Lifelong Learning: A Journal to Inform and Improve Practice*, 6 (2): 16–24.

Lebor, M. (2016), 'So What Do Managers Say About Disruptive Students?' *Journal of Further and Higher Education*, 40 (4): 568–583.

Lebor, M. (2017), *Classroom Behaviour Management in the Post-School Sector: Students and Teacher Perspectives on the Battle against Being Educated*, Basingstoke: Palgrave MacMillan.

Marzano, R., Marzano, J., and Pickering, D. (2003), *Classroom Management That Works: Research-Based Strategies for Every Teacher*, Alexandria, VA: Association for Supervision and Curriculum Development.

Mason, J. (2002), *Researching Your Own Practice: The Discipline of Noticing*, London: Routledge.

Mitchell, C., Pride, D., Haward, L., and Pride, B. (1998), *Ain't Misbehavin'*, London: Further Education Development Agency.

NIACE (2012), *Managing Challenging Behaviour within Skills Provision for Unemployed Adults*, Leicester: National Institute of Continuing Adult Education.

Parr, C. (2018), 'TES Talks to … Brian Nosek', *Times Educational Supplement*, 15 June: 42–44.

Parry, D., and Taubman, D. (2013), *UCU Whole College Behaviour Management: Final Report*, June 2013, London: UCU.

Petrie, J. (2015), 'Introduction: How Grimm Is FE', in M. Daley, K. Orr and J. Petrie (eds), *Further Education and the Twelve Dancing Princesses*, 1–12, London: IOE/Trentham.

Petty, G. (2006), *Evidence Based Discipline and Classroom Management*. Available online: http://geoffpetty.com/geoffs-books/downloads-for-ebt/ (accessed 3 November 2008).

Petty, G. (2018), *Supported Experiments*. Available online: http://geoffpetty.com/for-team-leaders/supported-experiments/ (accessed 16 June 2018).

Pinnegar, S., (1998) Introduction to part II: Methodological perspectives. In: M.L. Hamilton (Ed.), *Reconceptualizing teaching practice: Self-study in teacher education*, London: Falmer. pp 31–33.

Savage, S. (2016), *Exploring Video Observations of Classroom Practice through the Lens of Participant Observation*, ARPCE 8–10 July 2016, Oxford: ARPCE.

Schön, D. (1983), *The Reflective Practitioner: How Professionals Think in Action*, London: Temple Smith.

Stenhouse, L. (1979), 'Research as a Basis for Teaching', in *Inaugural Lecture by Lawrence Stenhouse*, Norwich: University of East Anglia.

Stenhouse, L. (1981), 'What Counts as Research', *British Journal of Educational Studies*, 29 (2): 103–114.

Vizard, D. (2012), *How to Manage Behaviour in Further Education*, 2nd edn, London: Sage Publications Ltd.

Wallace, S. (2014), 'When You're Smiling: Exploring How Teachers Motivate and Engage Learners in the Further Education Sector', *Journal of Further and Higher Education*, 38 (3): 346–360.

Wilby, P. (2013), 'The OECD's Pisa Delivery Man', *The Guardian*, 26 November. Available online: https://www.theguardian.com/education/2013/nov/26/pisa-international-student-tests-oecd (accessed 4 June 2018).

Wubbels, T., Brekelmans, M., van Tartwijk, J., and Admiral, W. (1999), 'Interpersonal Relationships between Teachers and Students in the Classroom', in H.C. Waxman and H.J. Walberg (eds), *New Directions for Teaching Practice and Research*, 151–170, Berkeley, CA: McCutchan.

7 How to Improvise Decisions in the Face of Disorder

SANDRA RENNIE

Introduction

There is an extensive range of practical strategies used by teachers to manage behaviour. Some of these may result from reasoned, reflective thought, some may be informed by training or behaviour management theories and others may be strategies formed out of habit or modelled on memories of our own previous teachers. This chapter does not aim to argue for, or justify, particular strategies. Instead it presents a model of teachers thinking for themselves and responding in real-life learning situations, to group dynamics, to patterns of behaviour and to their physical environment. It showcases the application of a framework theory and gives examples of how this approach can help teachers select workable strategies while at the same time continue to maintain flexibility in dealing with problem behaviours. The case studies used are all based on real situations with the names and some of the details changed to protect anonymity. The practical effectiveness of some 'top tips' for behaviour management, as described in Chapter 4, is examined in the light of the demands of these real teaching situations. Such behaviour management tips can present helpful guidance, especially for new teachers; however, when the unexpected occurs or when patterns of poor behaviour become entrenched in the classroom, such tips may become irrelevant clichés. This is because behaviour 'tips' provided by others do not fit the learning context or the organizational culture of the college or school, or they simply do not work at the particular time the teacher deploys them. It can be a frustrating and self-defeating process to randomly try one behaviour management strategy after another to deal with the class that is causing you to 'tear your hair out'. This chapter provides a theoretical framework, the Cynefin framework, to enable teachers to analyse their behaviour management problems and make informed decisions about how they will respond in certain types of situations.

The Cynefin framework – for decision-making

Cynefin is 'a Welsh word which translates as "place" or "habitat"' (Mindtools 2018), but it also includes many more layers of meanings such as 'home' and 'belonging' so this is not a complete and direct translation. Most behaviour management strategies are couched in terms of personal relationships between the teacher and the students; so, their exponents aim to see how these individual relationships can be improved, for example by the teacher being more assertive or more consistent in what they say and do. In this chapter we will look instead at the effect that the 'learning habitat' has on behaviour. A 'learning habitat' includes the culture of an organization, established custom and practice, the students' and teachers' backgrounds and cultures, the physical environment and the traditions and accepted practices of the subject being taught. The Cynefin framework (Snowden and Boone 2007) is a management theory that can be just as easily applied to the classroom as to the business world. It is a 'sense-making framework' that helps us to explore what is going on when we need to make decisions to act in particular habitats. It helps us recognize the patterns of behaviour emerging in front of us as and when they emerge. The framework describes the four different decision-making domains that managers (and teachers) might find themselves in: the Obvious domain; the Complicated domain; the Complex domain; and the Chaotic domain. When confronted with disorder, if we have not made sense of the domain in which the learning experience is playing out, our decisions will be based on our own pre-existing preferences and we will respond to poor behaviour in a habitual way, the way our own teachers responded to us in the past, or else we will resort to following 'tips' from behaviour 'gurus'. When these preferred methods fail to stem the disorder, we need to accept such approaches are not working and look for further ideas to help us develop alternative ways of thinking and acting.

The Obvious (simple) domain: sense–categorize–respond

In the Cynefin framework, the Obvious domain is one where the relationship between cause and effect is ordered and can be predicted in advance. In the classroom this occurs when there is one correct way of doing things and the teacher is expected to follow best practice in this and when relating with learners. To make the best decisions in the Obvious domain you need to 'sense' what is going on, 'categorize' the causes of this activity and choose your responses based on the categories identified. For example, consider a music teacher tasked with teaching a group of students the skill of playing their musical instruments together. This is likely to be an Obvious (simple) domain as playing in a concert band has an established structure and fixed traditions of behaviour. The student musicians each have their part to play, they have their sheet music to follow and the task of the teacher is to make sure they all follow the instructions written in the music, play in time to the conductor's beat and make music harmoniously together. The advice to follow in an Obvious domain like this is that the skilled teacher should be vigilant and open to what is happening in the classroom, that is, have 'withitness' (Kounin 1970) and when disorder arises the teacher can quickly categorize it into one of the regularly occurring categories they are familiar with in this type of class and respond accordingly. Here is an example of a 'top tip' in action and an example of a teacher following the process of making decisions in the Obvious domain.

Example A: top tip – give step-by-step instructions that are not open to misinterpretation

This case occurs in an instrumental music class with students, representing a variety of skill levels, learning to play a concert piece together. During the break time two of the participating students are overheard discussing the way the teacher talks when handling the class. One remarks:

> There is always background noise. Sometimes the teacher says 'shush' or 'be quiet'. This doesn't work with the group. They carry on. Sometimes the teacher says, 'You need to put your instruments down, look at me and listen carefully while I go through this next part'. This does work. If that works, why doesn't she do that all the time?

This is the kind of teachers' tip offered by Cowley (2014). The tip advises us that if you give detailed, clear instructions the students will follow them and if you give a generalized instruction to desist from doing something then students will often appear to ignore you as they have not instead been told clearly what they should do.

After the break the class restarts and once again there are background conversations causing a low-level disruption to learning. So instead of just saying 'shush', the teacher using the Cynefin framework will stop to think, observe that the musicians are not focused and become aware that this is because there are meaningful conversations going on rather than generalized chatting. The teacher then 'categorizes' these conversations. In this case it becomes obvious that the more skilled musicians are trying to explain the sheet music to the struggling students. Or perhaps, at another time, the teacher may observe that one student has just had a birthday party and is excitedly describing it to others nearby, or it may be that the students have just caught sight of a visitor peering through the glass door behind the teacher's back and so the alert teacher follows their gaze and spots the cause of the disruption. The teacher quickly categorizes in her own mind the reasons for the chatter as, for example, educational, social or practical and then their choice of response becomes self-evident. In the first case, where fellow students are having conversations about the music they are learning, and the conversations are educational, the teacher will allow time for paired work with the skilled and unskilled students sitting together. In the other case, they may respond to the social dynamics of the conversation by asking the students to play 'Happy Birthday' together on their musical instruments or if the interruption is an outsider they will take practical action and send a trustworthy student out of the room to welcome the visitor inside, so they can resume instructions to the class without background noise.

The Complicated domain: sense–analyse–respond

In a Complicated domain there are several diverse ways of doing things – all of which may be reasonable and effective. There are also several sources of information to help inform your decision. This multiplicity of information sources and potential solutions is what makes it complicated and mean the behaviour management decisions take more time. In a complicated situation, as well as exercising their authority and power confidently, the teacher needs to be well informed about the issues, the culture and background of the students, the policies of the organization and, ideally, to have access to expert advice to help solve the problem. Unlike the Obvious domain the response to an incident of disorder is not self-evident.

A top tip that many behaviour management theorists advocate is to set the ground rules at the beginning of a course and stick to them. These rules should be easy to understand and should be made public, so all are aware of them, for example on a poster displayed on the classroom wall. One tip proffered by Wallace is that such classroom rules 'should be few in number so they can be easily remembered' (2017b: 48). These rules may be negotiated at the beginning of a course with the students or they may be imposed by the teacher or, in the case of non-negotiable rules like health and safety, they may be imposed by the management. Whichever method is used to decide the rules, it is argued, the key factors are that they are understood, are memorable and are revisited when necessary. This sounds straightforward but, although remembering the words of written rules is easy, understanding the implications of these rules is more complicated. For example, one common rule on wall posters is that people should 'respect each other' and yet a difficulty with this rule is that there can be many different interpretations of this phrase, 'respect each other', varying from 'do what the teacher says' to 'demonstrate that you value diverse cultures and lifestyles'. It is important to express rules behaviourally as that reduces misunderstanding. Rogers (2015: 44) gives an example of doing this:

> To show respect in our classroom we are courteous, and we use our manners. We use positive language with each other. This means no teasing or put-downs. Bullying will never be tolerated.

When an unexpected disruption occurs, the teacher in a 'Complicated' domain, as defined by the Cynefin framework, needs to gather in the data, consult the experts, analyse the issues and only then finally make an appropriate response, as is demonstrated in the following example.

Example B: top tip – agree ground rules at the start and then apply them

The mentor of a trainee teacher was observing the teacher in an ESOL (English for Speakers of Other Languages) class. The trainee teacher had established a few ground rules at the beginning of the class, including one written on the whiteboard saying, 'respect each other'.

Towards the end of this well-managed and productive lesson, a couple of visitors knocked on the classroom door and walked into the room without invitation. They introduced themselves to the class as teachers of a free (i.e. funded) Basic Skills course that was being held elsewhere in the building. They were visiting to recruit new students for their next course. After introductions one visitor said to an ESOL student:

> Your name is Shahnaz, well you'll have to change that if you join my course as we have two Shahnazs on the course already.

At this statement, amid general embarrassed laughter in the class, the mentor had thirty seconds to decide how to deal with this. The mentor was the designated expert in the room and was the person who knew the class, and the trainee teacher had previously discussed the ground rule of 'respect each other'. The trainee teacher turned around and looked to the mentor for help in making a response to this incident. During these few seconds, the mentor realized they must analyse this incident and the application of the appropriate organization policies and consider the pros and cons of intervening. This will take more than thirty seconds as the learning experience was operating in a Complicated domain. Ideally, the teacher needed to know how Shahnaz felt being talked to like this, but there was neither the time nor opportunity to do this privately. The mentor knew it was complicated because there was a range of statuses and job roles and even work organizations present in the room; there were teachers, trainee teachers, an experienced teacher mentor and adult students from several different cultures, speaking different languages and with different levels of English comprehension. The process to be followed in the Complicated domain is (1) sense, (2) analyse and (3) respond. The mentor's thought processes were reported in writing later as follows:

1 Sense – observe carefully and attempt to make sense of the incident:

- The visitor is making a joke to try and break the ice.
- The visitor is nervous and doesn't think a person's name is considered important to them.
- The visitor is a teacher who has a policy in her classroom of changing the names of students in order to suit her convenience.

2 Analyse the possible reasons for this:

- This is an experimental theatre and there is a candid camera recording peoples' reactions.
- The visitor is using a comment about an individual's name in order to assert her status and to exercise power over the students. That is, she appears to be 'a bully' (a person who habitually uses bullying tactics to control a social situation).

As the 'expert' in the room a mentor should examine the pros and cons of intervening in this situation – making sure that for every positive 'pro' there is also a reverse side of the coin to be considered as a 'con'. (See Tables 7.1 and 7.2 for the arguments considered for and against the mentor's intervention.)

What other information does the mentor need? They may know a lot of information about the teacher being observed, but they are not likely to know much background information in relation to the students present in the class. When observing a teaching placement in a training centre, this mentor is required by their employing organization not to intervene unless there are safeguarding or health and safety issues. Is this the policy they should follow now? Does the mentor need to know the details of the inclusion policy of the training centre they are visiting or is it sufficient to follow the agreed values of the professional teaching organization? Standard 5 of Professional Values and Attributes states

Table 7.1 What happens if the mentor does intervene? Arguments to be considered

Pros	Cons
The student Shahnaz's name will be acknowledged, singled out and respected.	The student Shahnaz's name will be singled out, and she will be embarrassed and possibly teased.
The trainee teacher will observe an instance of anti-inclusive language being challenged by the mentor. This would be a model of good, inclusive practice.	The trainee teacher has been designated as the person 'in charge' of this lesson. She will experience the mentor taking action instead of her and usurping her position.
The visitor will learn that the practice of changing people's names without their expressed consent is not allowed in this classroom.	The visitor will not understand any challenge that is made about their words.

Table 7.2 What happens if the mentor does not intervene? Arguments to be considered

Pros	Cons
The student Shahnaz may not have followed all the English spoken by the visitor and thus may not have understood that this comment was a 'put down'.	The student Shanaz will not learn about the value of inclusion and respect for others in the classroom.
The trainee teacher will experience the real effects of managing or not managing all the interactions in a classroom.	The trainee teacher will observe an instance of anti-inclusive language being left un-challenged by others in authority.
The visitor will leave in a few minutes and will have not recruited Shahnaz as a new student to her class – this is good if she is not a real teacher.	The visitor will continue to believe that it is acceptable to call her students by names other than their own names.

that we should value and promote social and cultural diversity, equality of opportunity, and inclusion (Education and Training Foundation 2014).

This implies a requirement to respect students' identities and to challenge disrespectful language. The visitor had introduced herself as a teacher and, as such, if she is a member of a professional teaching organization she should adhere to these professional values. The trainee teacher should know the inclusion policies of her teaching practice placement but may not have been properly inducted into the organization. The mentor will need to check this later. The roles and statuses of the visiting 'teachers' are unclear, so the mentor should advise the trainee teacher to check the procedures for admitting visitors to the class and see whether they had been followed. This is a lot of information to be checked and evaluated from a variety of sources, and it will take time to carry out such research. So, as it was a complicated situation, the mentor took no immediate action while these thought processes were swirling around. Then the incident escalated. While the trainee teacher was sitting quietly at the front of the class watching the situation unfold, the visitor stood up and strode across the classroom, and standing a metre or so away facing the individual student Shahnaz, leant forward into her personal space and said, 'So what name will you choose instead?' For the mentor, the aggressive body language of the visitor, the uncertain body language of both the trainee teacher and the ESOL student and the oppressive nature of the words spoken by the visitor added the necessary information to precipitate the decision-making process. They could more accurately categorize the emerging interaction as follows:

- It appears that the visitor is acting like a bully and showing lack of respect.
- The visitor is either not a real teacher or, if she is indeed employed as a teacher, she does not subscribe to a teacher's code of ethics.
- The trainee teacher does not see it as her role to intervene as there are at least two apparently more qualified teachers in the room.
- The ESOL student is being publicly harassed and her identity being questioned.

3 Respond

Put like this the decision to act becomes easier. The mentor intervened and publicly affirmed everyone's right to use their own real name and not be required to change their name for any reason. They also decided later to speak privately to the manager of the ESOL training centre to alert them to the fact that a potentially harassing incident had taken place in one of their classes.

There are several different ways and different time frames in which this situation could be dealt with and all of these are reasonable and effective. There is no one right way of dealing with it as this problem is unlikely to have been encountered previously. Your choice of what to do and when you do it needs to be a decision based on what you sense is happening and on the evidence you have gathered as the incident unfolds. When a situation is complicated, collecting data and analysing it before responding is far more effective than reacting immediately or following a set script for what can or cannot be said or done in any given situation.

The Complex domain: probe–sense–respond

A Complex domain, in the Cynefin framework, is a system without identifiable causality. It is unlike the Complicated system where there are many and different causes, but all are identifiable either by further research or by asking the participants for further information. The Complex domain exists when students' behaviours change over time with no discernible reason for the change. It is particularly evident in creative learning environments, in environments where initiative and innovation are encouraged or in unstructured groups or crowds.

Observing the apparently random behaviour in a crowd of students, we can see emergent and changing outcomes with students moving around each other like a murmuration of starlings. These are identifiable patterns of behaviour, but cause and effect can only be identified with hindsight. In a class operating in the Complex domain, the teacher's strategy should be to conduct mini fail-safe experiments to explore any emerging issues that are causing the disruption to learning. It may be that the disruption itself becomes part of the learning experience. Here is an illustration of how a displayed regulation becomes subverted or ignored by a Complex group, how different customs and habits emerge over time and how change emerges and adapts because of practical, personal and environmental considerations.

Example C: top tip – display the regulations clearly and ensure they are followed

At an afternoon swimming session at the local municipal baths, I saw a sign instructing swimmers to swim round the pool in a clockwise direction. There was also another sign saying that slow swimmers should give way to faster swimmers. These were the only two rules displayed. The twenty or so adult swimmers in the pool were people I recognized as having attended the same session at the same time each week for the last month. They were 'regulars' and none of them were following either of the two written instructions displayed but were instead swimming up and down the length of the pool and occasionally weaving in and out of each other when they encountered slower swimmers. The two pool attendants watched the swimmers attentively but neither of them stopped their progress nor did they insist they follow the written instructions.

In a similar manner, many education venues have the rule: 'Walk on the left on the stairs and don't run in the corridors.' This regulation is there to ease the passage of all people around the building and to ensure health and safety. In practice, though, however simple these rules may be, sometimes they are followed by all and sometimes not. There may be practical reasons why during a lunch-time crowd or during the rush of a five-minute lesson-change there is neither time nor space to walk on the left-hand side. A custom-and-practice model of behaviour emerges, and this is reinforced over time by the crowd and then the authority of the rule becomes diminished. Like the swimmers, the pool attendants know there are written rules posted in front of them, but they can see there is also a custom and practice governing behaviour in the pool. Given a choice, the wise swimmer follows the custom and practice of the group and thus, even though the rules are broken, conflict and collisions are avoided. Often there may be good reasons for ignoring the rules: the swimmers in the pool may find it generally more efficient; there are less confident swimmers who prefer to swim near the edge; there are shy swimmers who prefer to swim near those of their own gender in case they accidentally bump into a member of the opposite sex; there are friendly swimmers who wish to chat while they complete their swim routine; and there are determined swimmers who wish to swim at speed and improve their personal best. This approach of ignoring the rules may be an example of differentiation and effective learning at its best.

The swimming pool had developed its own complex culture and social dynamics over time. The regulation of this swimming pool was designed to ensure the safety and comfort of unstructured crowds of swimmers. This is a learning experience as much as, if not more, than following a teacher's instructions to swim up and down the length of the pool. These swimmers had developed their own group dynamic, and their speed, agility and ability ebbed and flowed as they practised their swimming. Many adult education leisure classes operate in a Complex domain in this way. I wanted to learn how established rule-breaking had become within this Complex domain, so I carried out an experiment to probe accepted behaviour. I followed the exact letter of the two rules posted on the walls of the swimming pool and this resulted in a couple of near collisions and attracted attention and criticism from one of the pool attendants. However, at the swimming session the next week, most of the swimmers were following the published circulation regulation of swimming clockwise round the pool.

Often the best learning about social interactions and creativity takes place within the Complex domain. This is because the Complex domain is constantly changing and adapting in order that learners and teachers can function effectively. In this complex environment teachers must take the initiative of changing and adapting in response to the changing circumstances. This approach is very different from the learning process experienced in the Complicated or Obvious domains, where following pre-existing rules or policies is an essential requirement of being a successful learner or teacher. Rules for behaviour regulation in educational institutions are planned and agreed on by management and teachers, sometimes with the democratic participation of a student council or because of evaluation feedback from students, but often they are solely decided by responsible managers trying to ensure that legislation is adhered to and risks and dangers are avoided. However, risk aversion does not sit well with good pedagogy, especially if the learning is supposed to be about creativity, innovation, personal development or social interaction. Teaching and learning in these areas, by their very nature, entail taking risks: social risks; personal risks; physical risks; and the risks of failing. The teacher's choice of behaviour management strategy in the Complex domain needs to accommodate risks present in the environment, albeit manageable risks. The teacher can effectively manage learners' behaviours by developing the habit of observing and listening to their surroundings and then improvising tests to establish which are the best tactics to improve or redirect their behaviour.

Lee (2018) discusses the views of several professional education leaders on how teachers should be creative and 'adapting amid the pressure'. To these educationalists, the purpose of education is one more of personal transformation rather than just the acquisition of knowledge and the ability to follow instructions. It follows therefore that the chosen methods of behaviour management for teachers should be based on valuing 'autonomy, creativity, adaptability and collaboration' (Lee 2018) and encouraging the promotion of 'resilience' and 'well-being' among teachers and learners rather than simple rule-following.

The Chaotic domain

When there is chaos in a classroom, according to the Cynefin framework the appropriate response is (1) act then (2) sense and then (3) respond. Act first is considered the correct approach as any firm action will immediately impose some structure on the chaos, and it is only after a certain amount of order has been imposed that the factors that preceded the chaos can be examined. Chaos cannot be planned for it can only be reacted to. In acting first and thinking later teachers or their managers may comfort themselves with the thought that, according to the Hawthorne effect, whatever intervention they choose in the classroom there is likely to be some improvement. This is because their students know they are being observed and we as humans require to be given any attention by other humans – preferably positive regard. The argument is made that because of the presence of an observer, any introduction of changes in practice will inevitably improve outcomes. The Hawthorne effect, originally named in 1930 and still included in management texts (Hindle 2008), describes how changes to a production process and the presence of an observer seemed to lead to an increase in productivity whatever those changes were.

Managing behaviour in either a Complex or a Chaotic situation requires skills in improvisation. The ability to improvise, as any jazz musician or any member of a 'comedy improv. troupe' will tell you, is not something that can be performed well without understanding, thought and much rehearsal. Rehearsing possible scenarios helps to provide us with a selection of actions to choose from, so, contrary to popular opinion, it is the skilled and reflective practitioner who is the best improviser – not the beginner who 'makes it up as they go along'. From birth we learn through observation, copying and improvisation but as we mature into adulthood, if we experience risk-taking resulting in negative consequences, we can become so risk-averse that we lose the ability to improvise.

A teacher's tip from Wallace (Winter 2017b: 30) recommends:

Stand by the door and greet your learners as they come in. Greet as many as you can by name. Look pleased to see them all. Personalise your welcome in a positive whenever you can.

This is a good tip, but the following example demonstrates how the best laid plans to start with a welcome can go astray in the face of chaos.

Example D: top tip – welcome learners as they arrive in class

This is an evening creative skills class attended by a group of adults representing a range of ages and some of them with disabilities that impact on their social skills and learning. The teacher is delayed by an incident elsewhere, so they arrive at the learning centre to find one student with Asperger's syndrome standing outside the building trembling visibly and in a state of distress. The student said he was afraid to go in because one of the other students was very drunk and he said, 'I didn't like drunk people. I don't know what they are going to do.' The teacher comforts him and assures him that it is the drunk student who should be banished outside, not him. The teacher then confidently accompanies the frightened student back into the building and walks with him into the classroom. There they find that the drunk student has already been removed to an adjoining classroom by a teaching colleague. The remaining students are hanging around in confused bunches, looking anxious. Eventually the drunk student is persuaded by the teaching assistant to leave by another exit and the teacher starts the class with a warm-up drama exercise, trying to resume normal practice as soon as possible as the students were clearly shaken by the incident. A few minutes later the drunk student appears outside the window banging hard on the glass pane trying to gain access. The students once more bunch up into protective knots and the student with Asperger's starts trembling and becomes tearful. According to the Cynefin framework, when you are in a Chaotic situation any action you take will make things better – almost irrespective of what that action is. This is because by acting you are providing leadership and structure to a disordered situation. On impulse, the teacher switched the lights off in the classroom so that the class could no longer be seen from outside and then led the students into an inner classroom to resume the lesson. There was no need to gather further information about what had occurred earlier before the teacher acted. There was no need to scan the faces or the behaviour of the students to pick up further clues about how they were feeling and at that stage there was no need to carry out a forensic investigation of who said what and who did what. The correct approach was to act first, impose order and then gather information and respond.

Summary and conclusion

In each of these four case studies the pre-planning of teachers or managers has failed to prevent disorder. The case studies illustrate that 'top tips' have limited utility in real-life situations. It is the unexpected and the unpredictable that cause the most challenging problems for teachers and learners. Personal initiative and improvising solutions are required of teachers every time they teach; however, these skills and abilities are not necessarily discussed, evaluated and reflected upon by either the student-teacher or their teacher-educators. It appears a section of skills in behaviour management is missing from some teacher training curriculum and professional development courses for teachers. Instead new teachers are given established strategies, fixed policies and 'top tips' to follow. A teacher's skill in improvisation can improve with practice, feedback and experience. Issues that arise in the Obvious domain require a teacher to learn the skills of being aware and to sharpen their listening and observation skills. When an issue is in the Complicated domain, the teacher should make sure they make a considered response rather than a quick response; they need to have well-honed research and thinking skills. If there is Chaos then almost any confident response will improve matters, only panic from the teacher will make things worse. When a situation is in the Complex domain, this is arguably the place where more and different learning takes place as learning, by its very nature, requires new thoughts and new behaviours. To improve the way in which we respond to Complex situations in the classroom, a teacher should practise carrying out fail-safe experiments to probe what is happening in a class. This involves practising using new ways of talking, new actions and new ways of thinking. This kind of improvisation is a skill that is taught currently in drama classes and through role-play practice – new teachers should have the opportunity to learn and rehearse these skills in a similar manner.

Activities

1 Consider a Complex situation you have encountered in your classroom. Describe exactly what you saw happening. Discuss with a colleague what fail-safe experiments might have been suitable to try out in that scene.

2 With at least two other colleagues, practise improvising your response to disruptive incidents that regularly happen, as follows:

(a) Choose one role and one emotion from this list and allocate it at random to each colleague:

Roles: student, teacher, teaching assistant, parent, employer

Emotions: angry, confused, shy, distressed, in pain, ecstatically happy

(b) Act out a scenario in your classroom. The scenario title is 'The first five minutes of the lesson'.

(c) Afterwards discuss what happened, why it happened and any ways the scene could have been a better learning experience for all.

3 Read *Frameworks for Thinking: A Handbook for Teaching and Learning* (Moseley et al. 2005). Choose a framework that works for you and practise developing your thinking skills.

References

Cowley, S. (2014), *Getting the Buggers to Behave*, 5th edn, London: Bloomsbury.

Education and Training Foundation (2014), 'Professional Standards for Teachers and Trainers in Education and Training'. Available online: https://set.et-foundation.co.uk/professionalism/professional-standards/ (accessed 14 January 2019).

Hindle, T. (2008), 'The Hawthorne Effect', *Economist*, 3 November. Available online: https://www.economist.com/node/12510632 (accessed 25 April 2018).

Kounin, J.S. (1970), *Discipline and Group Management in Classrooms*, New York: Holt, Reinhart and Winston.

Lee, J. (2018), 'Adapting Amid the Pressure', *Intuition*, Summer, 32: 12–14.

Mindtools Content Team (2018), *The Cynefin Framework*. Available online: https://www.mindtools.com/pages/article/cynefin-framework.htm# (accessed 16 June 2018).

Moseley, D., Baumfield, V., Elliott, J., Higgins, S., Newton, D., Miller, J., and Gregson, M. (2005), *Frameworks for Thinking: A Handbook for Teaching and Learning*, Cambridge: Cambridge University Press.

Rogers, B. (2015), *Classroom Behaviour*, 4th edn, London: Sage.

Snowden, D., and Boone, M. (2007), 'A Leader's Framework for Decision Making', *Harvard Business Review*, November. Available online: https://hbr.org/2007/11/a-leaders-framework-for-decision-making (accessed 9 July 2018).

Wallace, S. (2017a), *Behaviour Management, Getting It Right in a Week*, London: Critical Publishing.

Wallace, S. (2017b), 'Learning to Play by Rules', *Intuition*, Education and Training Foundation, Winter, 30: 30–31.

8 Reflective Practice, Restorative Practice and Trust in Behaviour Management

ELIZABETH NEWTON AND DENISE ROBINSON

Introduction

This chapter features an overview of the main reflective models used in teaching and how these bear upon behaviour management. It provides an example of one college where restorative practice has been used to improve behaviour. The emphasis in some approaches to behaviour has tended to be 'technical' in the sense that strategies are recommended which do not recognize the social and economic structures in which we as teachers operate nor indeed our personal values and how these might affect our judgements and responses in a given situation. While we argue that the personal is never merely personal, we can 'shine a light' on how the personal can be interpreted showing how issues of power and control reveal a wider social, economic and historical setting. Giddens (1991) argues that one of the underpinning themes of recent times (which he refers to as 'high modernity') is formation of one's identity (self-identity) which has been fundamentally altered by the mechanisms through which such self-identity is formed and how individuals, in their turn, influence social conditions. As an example, consider attitudes to various issues as the environment, abortion, marriage, access to higher education and so on; these are matters which not only shape our lives but we, as individuals, help to shape. The development of the commercial environment in which we live has resulted in a fundamental shift away from the local and traditional to the distributed and global. As such, Giddens claims, modern lives are high-risk in the sense that more aspects of our lives are influenced by institutions and factors over which we may feel we have little control; trust in this scenario is seemingly difficult to realize and so more valued. The relationship to the role of teacher and student is clarified in this respect; the teacher is not merely the imparter of knowledge and skills but a person who needs to be valued in terms of trust. One of the factors in behaviour and its 'control' is trust. Students need to regard the teacher as someone whom they can trust and probably, respect.

Reflective models

Teaching is a complex activity and each teaching situation is unique. In order to support development both trainees and experienced practitioners need to undertake reflection of their teaching. It is through reflective practice that teachers grow and improve their teaching; without this they will probably simply repeat the same mistakes and remain in a state of perplexity or misunderstanding about events and behaviour in the classroom. In understanding behaviour, teachers need to consciously employ one or several reflective models. There are many models of reflective practice, and Kolb's reflective experiential learning model (1984) and Gibbs's reflective cycle (1988) are examples that focused on breaking down the teaching activity to be examined by asking questions, formulating analyses and action planning to improve teaching for the future. Schön's work (1983, 1987, 1991), and the considerable contribution he made to our understanding of reflective practice, is typically included in teacher education, but it is often to later contributions by Tripp (1993) and Brookfield (1995, 2017) that we focus our attention in helping us to understand at a more profound level and enabling us to use the 'core reflection' to which Korthagen and Vasalos (2006) refers.

Schön – reflection-in-action and reflection-on-action

Essentially, reflection-in-action is almost a simultaneous consideration of how to act while in the moment, rather than standing back and thinking later. This is because there are always new and surprising incidents in teaching. Reflection-on-action is a post–incident activity where we analyse what we did in the moment, what we have learned and how we can improve our teaching in the future. Further work by Schön with Argyris (1978, 1996) identified a difference between single- and double-loop learning: single-loop learning where the basic framework and reference points are taken for granted as opposed to double-loop learning which critiques and challenges such frameworks and leads to greater insights for improved learning.

An example of the difference between single- and double-loop learning can be seen in behaviour in the classroom as follows: you have a student who consistently chatters and distracts others. Your response as a teacher has been to discipline the student ('stop talking') to end the distracting behaviour. However, this worked for a while but then the chatting started again. To move into double loop you would need to take a different approach to seek the reason why the student does not seem able to concentrate on the work. This might include a separate tutorial discussion with the student and discussions with other teachers who may have the same problem with this student. In undertaking this, you might find that the student has a problem at home which is distracting them or feel that they need to chat to demonstrate that they are popular (seeking attention). Your response thus needs to be different to simply verbally disciplining the student.

Korthagen (2004), Korthagen et al. (2006) and Korthagen and Nuijten (2017) – core reflection model

This model can be regarded as a development from Schön which moves into the personal and emotional domains and even into counselling. Core reflection allows focus on the inner core beliefs rather than the behaviour-orientated analysis, which tends to render a superficial approach resulting in 'quick fixes' and negative responses. If a teacher focuses merely on the concrete (this happened, why, and how can I change it) there is a tendency to focus on the negative (what went wrong) and in doing so, create an aura of distaste around reflection itself. In order to promote deeper reflection, Korthagen (2004) proposed an onion ring model which moves reflection from the external and behavioural aspects of the situation, through competencies, beliefs and identity, to one's mission. One's mission may be understood by the teacher or, indeed, may be submerged below many other objectives. For example, a personal mission may be to work with students who should have a second chance, but this may be buried below objectives such as earning a living or students achieving a high success rate. By converging on the inner core aspects of beliefs, identity and mission, the teacher (new or experienced) is free to explore feelings (emotions) as well as thinking (cognition) and wanting (motivation) in a balanced way. Having identified the ideal outcome and any limiting beliefs in a problematic teaching situation, the teacher is able to move beyond negativity. This facilitates the teacher to develop an awareness of how to operate autonomously and positively such that the teacher can move from the outer ring to the inner (mission) and then out again to render ideas about outcomes in a concrete manner. This can be a relatively long and difficult process particularly in the first attempts.

An example of how this might work can be seen in the following. In the previous example, the teacher discovers that the talkative student does not like the subject and that she only started the course because she was under pressure from her parents to do it. After some reflecting, the teacher appreciates that not only does this present a problem for her in terms of classroom behaviour, but it does not sit easily with her belief that learning should be enjoyable and fit with the individual student's life objective nor with her mission to enthuse students in her vocational area. However, she feels limited in that she doesn't think she has the experience to take this situation forward. Having acknowledged that this situation is upsetting at a personal level, she decides to move forward by approaching several more experienced practitioners to discuss possible approaches. This may not resolve the problem easily or quickly in the classroom but at least she understands the situation and she may be able to find ways of channelling the student's interest.

Tripp (1993, 2012) – critical incident analysis

Tripp has developed an approach to critical incident analysis which can be particularly useful in accessing the core and personal theories as described by Korthagen et al. (2006).

Although critical incident analysis (originally developed by Flanagan in 1954 for job analysis) explores a particular incident which may be something quite innocuous, through a process of asking 'why' and 'because' in relationship to the incident, the teacher is able to explore fundamental beliefs and perhaps challenge the assumed beliefs inherent in both professional and organizational practice. There are alternative thoughts about what constitutes a critical situation, with some considering a mundane incident which the teacher is curious about to be potentially just as useful as an unusual incident. It hopes to identify any fundamental issues that triggered such curiosity and leads the teacher to reflect upon it in a structured way and consider options for future actions. Critical in this sense does not imply negativity but a requirement to analyse, question and seek different perspectives, some of which may be challenging and result in a very different approach in relationship to behaviour strategies.

An example of how Tripp's work might be used is given by Mohammed (2016). She provides a case study of an incident in her classroom of a group of seemingly difficult trainee teachers who challenged the exercise she had asked them to undertake. Although these were motivated adults, intent on achieving a professional qualification, they were just as 'difficult' in this scenario as one might find with 16-year-olds in a vocational education and training (VET) setting. Her reflections are very revealing about her basic and underlying values which show that her focus was perhaps more concerned with her own objectives, rather than those of her students.

Brookfield – critical reflection and the four-lens model

In considering reflection as a tool in critical understanding, Brookfield highlights: 'Structures and forces present in the wider society always intrude into the classroom' (2017: 10) and that no teacher can ultimately control what happens in the classroom. Brookfield contrasted critical reflection to technical reflection as 'quite simply, the sustained and intentional process of identifying and checking the accuracy and validity of our teaching assumptions' (2017: 3). In other words, critical reflection is distinctive in that it requires us as practitioners to explore and critique at a deeper level and one which acknowledges that teaching and teachers are in a position of power, set within a dominant ideology. A critical perspective essentially illuminates power relationships including those that work against the interests of those who accept the prevailing ideology. This, according to Brookfield is pervasive, difficult to identify and even more difficult to oppose. It maintains inequality; from a critical theory perspective such an ideology is seen as a means of control 'designed to keep a fundamental unequal system safe from challenge' (2017: 13). On this basis the teacher becomes embroiled in the making and maintenance of such a system. The teacher also becomes limited by the institutional policies and practices which maintain the system. While teachers may express concern and even object to some aspects of institutional policies, they are ultimately bonded to their 'calling' as a teacher and will often devote much time and energy in protecting students from the deleterious effects (as perceived by the teacher) of such institutional policies. In order to work as a practitioner with such dilemmas, Brookfield has developed a 'four lens' model which can guide structured and critical thinking about teaching. The four lenses are just that: a way of analysing teaching from a particular position or vantage point. These are autobiographical (self); learners; colleagues; and finally, theory (literature from research). While Brookfield considers the autobiographical as a starting point, as this may expose assumptions previously unidentified, the exercise of moving into other perspectives opens possibilities not necessarily considered in the typical 'what, why, how' approach. It reveals the paradigmatic (basic assumptions not normally realized and which form part of our way of operating in the world), prescriptive (what we think ought to happen) and causal (how things work and relate to each other) assumptions. In typical reflections, the causal assumptions are the easiest to identify whereas the prescriptive and presumptive require in-depth reflective activities exposing what lies behind some common-sense assumptions.

An example of this model can be seen following from the the earlier case studies above. In taking up the plight of a student who displays disruptive behaviour as a result of being required to enrol on a course of little interest to them, there is considerable antipathy from other teachers on the basis that student numbers are required to keep the class viable and that without these numbers, the class will close or be merged with another and some of them could lose their jobs. There is a chance that if one student leaves, others may follow as there are a number who feel the same as this particular disruptive student. Some of the teachers articulate their fear quite openly, others justify their response by claiming that this is the best course for the student as there is nothing else suitable for them. The teacher is witnessing an unsatisfactory situation; the educational opportunities for this student are limited and that the teachers are merely looking to their job security.

Comments on the models

From a reading of these models we can see some common threads running through all of them. Essentially it is to improve one's teaching by analysing what we did in our teaching. Schön's work is a useful first step in reflective activity but in order to move beyond the merely concrete (and sometimes repetitive actions) a focus on core and assumptions that are often held and acted upon without acknowledgement can lead to much more effective and long-lasting improvements in practice. A different perspective is provided by Korthagen's approach by referencing the emotional and one's inner core beliefs; Tripp's focus on a critical incident supports reflection allowing us to concentrate on a specific teaching matter, while Brookfield's model supplies teachers with a deeper tool for analysis, incorporating wider social, structural as well as exposing and often challenging our underlying assumptions and values (Table 8.1).

The next section considers restorative practice and the use of restorative conversations as used in one college. This exemplifies a cross-college strategy which underpins a teacher–student relationship of trust.

Table 8.1 Comparing reflective models

Author	Model description	Main elements	Critique
Schön, 1983, 1987, 1991	Reflection-in-action and reflection-on-action	In the moment and post-incident analysis.	Limited to the concrete and short term; tendency to negativity.
Korthagen, 2004, Korthagen and Vasalos, 2006; Korthagen and Nuijten, 2017	Core reflection	Focus on core competencies, beliefs, identity and mission.	Focus is on the teacher; long and difficult process.
Tripp, 1993, 2012	Critical incident analysis	Exploring fundamental beliefs and assumptions through the analysis of an incident.	Little regard for societal structures, external factors or environment.
Brookfield, 1995, 2017	Critical reflection and the four-lens model	Teachers are in a position of power and control, set within a dominant ideology.	Focus on power dynamics may distract teacher from the practicalities of teaching.

Trust and restorative conversations

In recent years, various factors have precipitated a move away from strategies focused on behaviour management towards less punitive approaches to disruptive behaviour in the further education (FE) sector. In some institutions, an approach known as restorative practice has been implemented in an attempt to deal with discipline in a less negative manner. This discussion outlines the way in which restorative practice has been introduced into one large urban college in the UK and highlights progress and successes to date. Restorative practice has its roots in restorative justice, which is a way of bringing together the perpetrators and victims of crime in an attempt to heal wrongdoing. The practice of restorative justice was partly influenced by traditions from New Zealand's Māori customs and the way in which whole communities are involved in understanding and addressing misconduct (Kelly and Thorsborne 2014: 10). Its influence has spread to other countries including the United States and Canada, where it was used as 'a way of assisting offenders to take responsibility for their actions by helping them to understand and to repair the harm done to victims and their families' (Thorsborne and Blood 2013: 19). Thus, the wrongdoer becomes accountable for the harm they have caused, and both the perpetrator and the victims come together to rectify it and heal.

Within FE, factors that have led to the uptake of restorative practice as an alternative to disciplinary procedures include the success of this approach in the school sector. This is partly a result of the government's academies programme; as FE colleges become sponsors of multi-academy trusts, and as academy pupils begin to feed into FE colleges, approaches to behaviour in the secondary sector have begun to have an influence on FE. In addition, increased numbers of school-aged learners are now being educated in an FE setting; the closure of pupil referral units (PRUs) has led to a larger proportion of 14–16-year-olds being accommodated in alternative provision or academy settings within FE colleges. Among these learners, including some who have Education and Health Care Plans, are those who display emotional and behavioural difficulties. For this student cohort, behaviour management strategies such as behaviour contracts may not be wholly effective or appropriate. The cross-fertilization of behaviour policy from the school sector into FE stems from the realization currently gaining traction among both school and FE staff that punitive behaviour management can be ineffective and can, in some instances, lead to an escalation of disciplinary procedures, further poor behaviour and worsened working relationships with learners. Anecdotal evidence suggests that learners can end up in isolation – or worse, excluded – for what may initially have been a relatively minor infringement of institutional rules, such as forgetting to bring equipment to class. Learners' resentment at being punished for low-level failure to follow rules may fester and lead to further instances of poor behaviour, resulting in a ratcheting up of penalties and a vicious circle of infringement and punishment, accompanied by a deterioration in working relationships between staff and students.

Not only do strict behaviour management strategies affect levels of engagement within the education system, but there has been recognition internationally that exclusion from education leads to poor outcomes in learners' future lives. A conference held at the Harvard Graduate School of Education discussed 'zero tolerance' discipline approaches and their relation to the 'cradle to prison pipeline' (Sanghani 2012). This 'pipeline' concerns youths who have received custodial sentences. Their experiences of disciplinary procedures in education have resulted in '[the] unnecessary criminalization of non-violent behaviors [which] in some cases, nearly tripled the occurrence of suspensions and expulsions. The consequences of these punitive punishments can be dire. Students that are suspended in school are three times more likely to drop out, and students that drop out are three times more likely to end up in prison' (Sanghani 2012).

The picture in the UK, where over half of the prison population consists of individuals who were excluded from education, is similar. Vulnerable children are the hardest hit by exclusion, coming predominantly from disadvantaged families, having special educational needs, mental health needs or a disability, with black Caribbean children over-represented among those excluded (Weale 2017).

Inclusion

Promoting inclusion in education is a means of equalizing educational, social and cultural capital across socio-economic groups by enhancing life chances for those from less privileged backgrounds. The drive to encourage inclusion in education is championed by the United Nations Educational, Scientific and Cultural Organization (UNESCO), which supports Education for Sustainable Development. UNESCO is tasked with measuring progress towards targets on Education for Sustainable Development. One of its goals is to 'ensure inclusive and equitable quality education and promote lifelong learning opportunities for all' (UNESCO 2017: 18). Education for Sustainable Development includes a focus upon creating equal opportunities and promoting peaceful relations between people. This links to behaviour strategies that aim to involve and empower learners to make choices regarding behaviour, allowing them to remain active participants in education by resolving conflicts related to wrongdoing. Restorative practice offers a more productive alternative than policies that result in isolation or exclusion from peers and, potentially, a resentment of education. Education for Sustainable Development aims to enhance social cohesion, active citizenship, equity, justice and inclusivity, placing value on the non-economic and non-educational consequences of learning. In respect of inclusion, restorative approaches offer a potential solution. Restorative practice also supports the aims of Target 4.7: 'By 2030, ensure that all learners acquire the knowledge and skills needed to promote sustainable development, including, among others, […] promotion of a culture of peace and non-violence' (UNESCO [n.d.]). As the above quotation suggests, living in a community where individuals can coexist without friction is of key importance in education and globally.

Restorative practice: implementation in one FE college

With regard to how restorative practice can be implemented in FE, an example of the success of this approach is illustrated by the experience of one institution. The college in question is a large urban FE college, where a previous Ofsted inspection had raised concerns regarding behaviour, noting that teachers were having difficulty in managing classes, particularly in respect of low-level disruption. Ofsted's findings highlighted behaviour as an area upon which the college needed to focus, with the inspection report considering that the institution 'required improvement' with regard to learners' behaviour. There was a perceived need within the college to break away from managing behaviour in the same way as had been done historically, and from using the same language as had previously been used in disciplinary procedures, an approach which led repeatedly to the same negative results. The college sought to facilitate ways of repairing damage and opening communication channels between staff and learners and turned to models of restorative practice to do so.

The college sought examples of successful restorative practice from local schools, taking up the principles of restorative practice in a way it adapted to its own particular needs as an FE provider. This included respecting fairness, giving everyone a say and including everyone in college life. The principles of restorative practice were applied across the college, having been introduced to staff gradually. At the time of writing, 800 staff and 50 students have been trained in restorative practice methods, including security staff, executive board members, learning support assistants, teaching staff and representatives of the students' union. The training has consisted of restorative practice awareness sessions as well as some bespoke sessions for staff dealing with challenge and change.

The approach taken in this training is to place an emphasis on communication, emphasizing the fact that everyone has triggers or flashpoints that may be sparked by particular stressors. The training also highlights that the way in which humans respond in stressful situations can be disproportionate. As a starting point, teaching staff have been asked to establish a routine of 'check-ins' and 'check-outs' with learners at the beginning and end of every teaching session or tutorial. This is a means of allowing the teacher to gauge the tone of the room at the start of each session by asking individuals what is on their mind, helping teachers to ascertain the mood and feelings of their learners. This, for some learners, may be a chance to express feelings that may relate to life outside college that would otherwise go unmentioned and be repressed (perhaps only to erupt later). By externalizing their feelings at the outset, they can then put these feelings aside for the duration of the session. As the session ends, there is a chance to 'check out' and for learners to return to considerations of home or social life.

Teaching practitioners have been asked to consider how they deal with basic conversations in respect of adapting their behaviour and language, so as to avoid judging and assuming. One of the main foci of the training offered to staff within this college deals with the way in which staff use language to communicate with learners and develop a means of effective dialogue about what went wrong and what could happen to repair harm when incidents of misbehaviour occur. Part of the aim of this is to develop in learners the resilience to recover when situations go wrong. The tutor's role here is to help learners deal with any perceived unfairness. In the college being described, when events take a negative turn, they are dealt with by stopping the session being taught if necessary and beginning a restorative conversation. This may involve speaking to learners about what constitutes adult behaviour and supporting them to understand that the aim of the discussion is to create a safer environment for all. During a restorative conversation, learners and staff explain what is important to them or what their triggers are. This may include individuals expressing to the community around them (their classmates, peers and teachers) what they would like others to do, or not to do, in stressful situations. This helps groups to support each other and to build a sense of community. Thus, the community can recognize what each individual needs to help them to cope in stressful situations and to deal with what goes wrong in a way that safeguards both staff and learners. A teacher may say to learners, for example, 'When I see you two shouting at each other, it makes me worried about your safety.' This approach ensures that learners understand that the teacher is not blaming either party but is expressing concern for both of them.

Another key aspect of this process is to deal with the problem, rather than the person; to seek out the facts about what has happened, rather than who is to blame. The teacher's role is to listen and use engaging language. Engaging language in this college forms the framework of the restorative conversation. The college produced a set of questions as a 'script' or toolkit to guide teachers' conversations with learners. The aim was to avoid a situation in which staff shouted or used negative language and consciously sought to avoid this in their decision-making when having conversations with learners. The script has been issued to staff in the form of a card to keep on their staff lanyard as an *aide-mémoire* to support them to structure restorative conversations as the need arises. The framework consists of five questions as follows:

- What happened?

    1 How did this make you feel at the time?
    2 How does it make you feel now?
    3 What needs to happen to move this forward after this meeting?
    4 When can this be reviewed?

Having allowed the parties involved to state what happened, or to describe the issue that occurred, they will then verbalize how this made them feel at the time of the incident. For example, during one restorative conversation, a learner who had been present when another threw a chair over in class expressed her terror at witnessing the event. This was a powerful revelation to the chair thrower, who had been so wrapped up in his/her own feelings that he/she had not considered the impact of his/her actions on others present. The effect of this was to make the chair thrower cognizant of other parties' feelings. After this, the participants in the conversation express their current feelings. The next stage is for the parties concerned to say what needs to happen next, for example in a case where a learner may be harassing a peer via social media, this may be: 'I need her to stop messaging me on Facebook.' This is followed by an agreement as to when the discussion can be reviewed; such interventions need to be followed up. At the review, the teacher may comment on changed behaviours: 'I have noticed that you are not yelling at each other any more in the corridors.' 'I saw you helping her in class the other day; well done.'

The restorative process also aims to make teachers reflect more generally on communication and on how they deal with people. This involves a certain level of emotional intelligence, with teaching staff considering the learners' perspective: What is it that makes learners want to come through the door? The personal connections involved in making learners feel they belong to a community, and in developing relationships with staff and other students, are key in this regard. The practical application of restorative practice is in developing emotional intelligence and resilience in staff and students.

Outcomes

The effect of the training has been that staff have reported being better equipped to address potentially unstable situations. Additionally, they have noticed differences in respect of the outcomes of the interventions they have had with their learners and are now more able to respond in a balanced way. This means according attention not just to negative aspects of learners' behaviour but also to small developments or successes and addressing issues in a way that focuses on finding resolutions. Among some groups of learners, staff have overheard restorative conversations occurring spontaneously, with learners asking each other questions from the script their teachers have used with them.

The college's senior management team has now fully committed to restorative practice, placing it at the centre of working relationships college-wide, at all levels. While it is difficult, if not impossible, to attribute the result of such a programme of training in an institution which is implementing numerous improvement strategies, at the time of publication, the most recent Ofsted inspection awarded an 'outstanding' rating to personal development, behaviour and welfare. This represented a considerable improvement on the 'requires improvement' rating only two years previously. A second year of awareness training in restorative practice is forthcoming, with a focus on bespoke training sessions. This aims to focus on areas within the college where restorative practice can further support stronger, more resilient and fairer relationships.

Critique

It could be argued that restorative practice has several shortcomings, not least of which is the perception on the part of students who are well behaved that their misbehaving classmates are 'getting away with' poor behaviour and that their 'punishment' is no worse than having to sit down and talk through the consequences of their behaviour. The misbehaving learners themselves might also view the situation in this light and continue to behave in the same way. If the restorative process 'fails', should this result in a return to punitive behaviour management? Restorative practice could also be viewed a reactive, rather than a proactive process, in which situations are only dealt with after the event; relationships are repaired and reconciliations occur post-wrongdoing. Critics may argue that a proactive approach to behaviour could be more effective in heading off issues before they arise (Table 8.2).

Table 8.2 An overview of reflective practice

Author	Model description	Main elements	Critique
Thorsborne and Blood, 2013	Restorative practice	Alternative to 'behaviour management'; involves having a restorative conversation to discuss the effects of wrongdoing, rather than punishing the wrongdoer.	'Punishment' is too 'light' and may encourage repeat offending. The process is reactive rather than proactive.

Conclusions

Above all, this chapter highlights that reflective models can be used to develop a stronger base from which to apply appropriate strategies as outlined in this book. These models include how values and structural issues can affect teaching and learning. It is crucial that trainee teachers and teachers themselves move beyond a 'quick-fix' approach to reflection to effect good teacher–student relationships based on trust. The restorative conversations used in one FE college demonstrate how this can be done and the positive outcomes demonstrate its effectiveness. The fact that this project was introduced and developed through cross-fertilization from practice in the school sector demonstrates how partnerships between schools and FE colleges can lead to improvements previously not considered to be possible. Trust, again, is regarded as a constant feature of good behaviour management.

Activities

1   Consider a piece of reflection you have previously completed or one that you are about to complete. Re-analyse or analyse it in terms of the four models: Schön, Korthagen, Tripp and Brookfield. What are the differences in the processes and the identified outcomes of the models? Which works for you?

2   Restorative justice and conversations may need to be applied across a whole college to be effective. However, can you identify how you might be able to apply within your course or class? How might this work?

References

Argyris, C., and Schön, D.A. (1978), *Organizational Learning: A Theory of Action Perspective*, Reading, MA: Addison Wesley.

Argyris, C., and Schön, D.A. (1996), *Organisational Learning II: Theory, Method and Practice*, Reading, MA: Addison-Wesley.

Brookfield, S. (1995), *Becoming a Critically Reflective Teacher*, 1st edn, San Francisco, CA: Jossey-Bass.

Brookfield, S. (2017), *Becoming a Critically Reflective Teacher*, 2nd edn, San Francisco, CA: Jossey-Bass.

Flanagan, J.C. (1954), 'The Critical Incident Technique', *Psychological Bulletin*, 51 (4): 327–358.

Gibbs, G. (1988), *Learning by Doing: A Guide to Teaching and Learning Methods*, Oxford: Further Education Unit, Oxford Brookes University.

Giddens, A. (1991), *Modernity and Self-identity: Self and Society in the Late Modern Age*, Cambridge: Polity.

Kelly, V.C., and Thorsborne, M. (2014), *The Psychology of Emotion in Restorative Practice*, London and Philadelphia: Jessica Kingsley.

Kolb, D.A. (1984), *Experiential Learning: Experience as the Source of Learning and Development*, Englewood Cliffs, NJ: Prentice Hall.

Korthagen, F.A.J. (2004), 'In Search of the Essence of a Good Teacher: Towards a More Holistic Approach in Teacher Education', *Teaching and Teacher Education*, 20 (1): 77–97.

Korthagen, F., and Vasalos, A. (2006), 'Levels in Reflection: Core Reflection as a Means to Enhance Professional Growth', *Teachers and Teaching*, 11 (1): 47–71.

Korthagen, F., Loughran, J., and Russell, T. (2006), 'Developing Fundamental Principles for Teacher Education Programmes and Practices', *Teaching and Teacher Education*, 22 (8): 1020–1041.

Korthagen, F., and Nuijten, E. (2017), 'Core Reflection Approach in Teacher Education', *Oxford Research Encyclopedia of Education*. Available online: http://education.oxfordre.com/view/10.1093/acrefore/9780190264093.001.0001/acrefore-9780190264093-e-268 (accessed 6 June 2018).

Mohammed, R. (2016), 'Critical Incident Analysis: Reflections of a Teacher Educator', *Research in Teacher Education*, 6 (1): 25–29.

Sanghani, P. (2012), 'Let's Talk: Restorative Justice Practices', *Harvard Graduate School of Education*, 12 May. Available online: https://www.gse.harvard.edu/news/12/05/lets-talk-restorative-justice-practices (accessed 26 June 2018).

Schön, D. (1983), *The Reflective Practitioner: How Professionals Think in Action*, London: Temple Smith.

Schon, D.A. (1987), *Educating the Reflective Practitioner: Toward a New Design for Teaching and Learning in the Professions*, San Francisco, CA: Jossey Bass.

Schon, D.A. (1991), *The Reflective Practitioner*, Aldershot: Ashagate Publishing Ltd.

Thorsborne, M., and Blood, P. (2013), *Implementing Restorative Practices in Schools*, London and Philadelphia: Jessica Kingsley.

Tripp, D. (1993), *Critical Incidents in Teaching: Developing Professional Judgement*, London: Routledge.

Tripp, D. (2012), *Critical Incidents in Teaching: Developing Professional Judgement*, London and New York: Routledge Falmer.

UNESCO (2017), *Education for Sustainable Development Goals*. Available online: http://unesdoc.unesco.org/images/0024/002474/247444e.pdf (accessed 26 June 2018).

UNESCO (n.d.), *Learning to Live Together Sustainably (SDG4.7): Trends and Progress*. Available online: https://en.unesco.org/themes/gced/sdg47progress (accessed 26 June 2018).

Weale, S. (2017), 'School Exclusions Data in England Only "the Tip of the Iceberg"', *The Guardian*, 10 October. Available online: https://www.theguardian.com/education/2017/oct/10/school-exclusion-figures-date-england-only-tip-iceberg (accessed 26 June 2018).

9 Ethos and Culture across the Compulsory and Post-Compulsory Sectors and Its Impact on Behaviour Management

JOANNE IRVING-WALTON

Introduction

Increasingly, initial teacher education (ITE) and teaching career pathways are no longer as firmly delineated by sector as they once were. This is underpinned by a movement in policy towards supporting greater flexibility within the education workforce. Changes to statutory qualification requirements have had an impact; Qualified Teacher Status (QTS) and Qualified Teacher Learning and Skills (QTLS) (DfE 2014) now have parity and there is increased flexibility around employment in non-maintained schools (DfE 2018). Notably the requirement for all students to be in education or training until 18 is impacting the compulsory/post-compulsory boundary and with it the perceived roles of schools and further education (FE). Likewise, challenges linked to teacher recruitment across sectors have also played their part in the development of novel solutions and creative approaches to meeting the needs of local areas. Within this wider context, schools and FE colleges are responding with greater flexibility in relation to their curricula; the ways that students access learning that meets their needs; who is employed; and the ways in which staff are employed.

It may be the case that clear sector identities remain, and old inter-sector rivalries persist, but as the statutory dividing lines between compulsory and non-compulsory education continue to blur, it is natural, and desirable, that levels of integration, staff mobility and cross-sector working will increase rather than diminish.

In many ways approaches to learning, teaching, assessment, leadership and management in schools and FE have clear similarities and make integration seem a straightforward process, but it would be disingenuous to suggest that moving from one environment to another does not require adaptation; behaviour management in particular is an area that can seem most unfamiliar to teachers who transition between sectors. Further to this, with greater integration there also comes the tendency to transfer practice and there is a danger that approaches common to one sector are replicated without a clear consideration of the unique characteristics of the other. Quite simply, the recognition and preservation of the unique characteristics of sectors is something that should be encouraged and applauded; diversity in provision, after all, supports variety in student needs, and differences in approach to behaviour management are core to meeting those needs.

What this means for teachers across sectors is that in ITE and professional enhancement, it is increasingly desirable to develop a clear understanding of sector differences to support day-to-day working and career progression. In this chapter, therefore, the role of ethos and culture in relation to behaviour management will be approached from the position of the compulsory sector and compared to current practice and inspection process within the post-compulsory sector.

Ethos and culture

It is a very simple statement, but no two schools are the same, nor do they remain static in their characteristics. They feel different, they have different approaches, unique atmospheres and they promote, often overlapping, sets of values in divergent ways. While this is the case for any educational institution this individuality in characteristics has particular impact within the compulsory sector. In contrast to other institutions, schools, regardless of their type, size or phase, are by nature small but intensely connected communities of staff, students and parents who operate in very close proximity, in highly defined patterns, over significant periods of time. Schools also tend to occupy disproportionately recognizable physical, and metaphorical, spaces for the young people, families and communities that they serve becoming embedded formative features in the lives of individuals and collective groups. It is no wonder, then, that from this position schools naturally develop, and actively seek to project, institutional identities that are visible and recognizable.

This overarching sense of identity, tone and spirit is referred to as the school ethos or culture. In a sense the ethos and culture of a school reflect and embrace its outlook, values, beliefs, atmosphere and ideals. Indeed, it has been suggested that the concept of ethos can only be made intelligible through its connection to more tangible terms such as 'ambience' and 'atmosphere' (Allder 1993) and that it can be viewed as emerging from institutional culture (Solvason 2005), where culture refers to a school's shared patterns of behaviour and jointly negotiated relationships (Policy First 2010).

Ethos and culture are powerful and pervasive concepts within schools and institutions, able to simultaneously replicate, underpin and direct aspects of practice and all manner of relationships. It is common for schools and colleges to advertise constructed statements of their ethos and culture, statements that are used to provide a collective vision which neatly conveys the intended spirit and defining features of the organization. In many ways the compulsory and post-compulsory sectors overlap considerably in their practice. However, the ways in which the visible culture and ethos of schools are conceived are quite different to the more corporate approaches to these concepts adopted by large FE institutions which undertake multiple functions, serve several roles and derive income from a variety of revenue streams.

However, ethos within schools and colleges exists on multiple levels (Donnelly 2000) and while a recurring concept in policy, ethos is also nebulous defying straightforward definition, evaluation or application (McLaughlin 2005). Furthermore, ethos can be positive or negative in its impact. It may inspire and increase aspiration or create a toxic environment that perpetuates chronic underachievement. Nonetheless, ethos is a concept that permeates multiple aspects of practice in schools and colleges and should be considered when discussing approaches to leadership, learning and teaching, staff development and the creation of a positive learning environment and effective behaviour management systems (Bennett 2017).

Behaviour in schools: what is it really like?

Behaviour in schools is an emotive and complex area capable of eliciting extreme responses from educational professionals, students and the general public alike. It is not uncommon to hear behaviour categorized in the dichotomous and unhelpful terms of good or bad or for entrenched views around behaviour to be shaped by a handful of personal experiences. Likewise, violent incidents, falling standards and disruptive classrooms are perennially news-worthy, often creating a picture of an education system at the perpetual brink of crisis.

The shifting sands of education add to this sense of volatility. The relative roles of parents, society and schools in instilling standards of behaviour and values in young people are increasingly blurred (McKenzie 2014). While increasing calls for schools to address areas beyond the core academic curriculum, the increase in the use of technology and social media (Zych et al. 2015) and concerns around the well-being and mental health of students (DoH and DfE 2017) all play their part in adding to the complexity of an already wide-ranging area.

However, while perceptions of behaviour in schools can vary considerably often veering towards negative extremes the reality is perhaps infinitely more balanced. Bennett (2017) in evaluating a range of available evidence suggests that most of the time, in most schools, most students behave appropriately. However, this report also suggests that on balance there is a problem with the overall standard of behaviour in our schools and improvements can be made. There is no crisis but there is inconsistency both within and across institutions.

An area of interest within the evidence reported by Bennett (2017) are the attitudes of teachers towards behaviour management. Notably a picture is painted of behaviour management as an area ignored within the continuing professional development (CPD) cycle which is compounded by a dichotomy between the negative views of classroom teachers and the positive outlook of institutional leadership. This perhaps indicates a tendency towards poorly conceived whole-institutional approaches that rely on their development and drive being implemented and enforced through an authoritarian, top-down approach rather than a facilitative approach that includes staff, students and other stakeholders. When considering ethos and culture this is particularly significant since these concepts do not only relate to the experience of students but to the whole institution and all its staff. A strong ethos, culture and vision provide staff with clarity, support and a sense of connection resulting in a stronger sense of professional purpose (Policy First 2010).

In recent years education policy in England has increased its focus on the quality of behaviour within schools. The Department for Education (2016) has issued strengthened guidance on the rights of teachers in dealing with disruptive behaviour and has provided clearer expectations for the content and focus of statutory school discipline policies. Further to this the tightening of standards within the inspection framework (Ofsted 2015) around behaviour management has led, unsurprisingly, to a more concentrated focus around this area. This strengthened emphasis links behaviour to welfare, learning and the experiences of students within the school environment mirroring in many ways the same emphasis within FE frameworks (Ofsted 2016). However, there is a core difference. In schools responsibility lies squarely with the institution to create, manage, develop and instil appropriate behaviour. In FE there is a greater acknowledgement of learner autonomy; the efficacy of systems needs to be evidenced but students take greater responsibility for engaging with and contributing to those systems.

This is nothing more than a simple snapshot of the current position of behaviour management within schools. It should be remembered that any discussion of behaviour is contextually dependent; schools work in varying circumstances, attitudes to behaviour is subjective and the ways in which current government data is collected is open to critique. Yet while the challenges faced by schools and colleges may be variable there is common ground and it is possible for schools and colleges, in even the most challenging circumstances, to provide environments for their students that are safe, supported and encourage high quality learning to take place.

Behaviour management in schools and FE: same but different

Across education much is made of the differences between sectors and phases. There exists a real sense of cultural separation that can lead to broad-brush generalizations and misconceptions from all sides. Yet for individual teachers there is the possibility to benefit both professionally and personally from the ability to move between sectors throughout the course of their working lives.

In many ways approaches to behaviour management in the compulsory and post-compulsory sector overlap considerably particularly in relation to the nuts and bolts classroom-level strategies employed to build positive learning environments and manage disruption. After all many of the fundamentals required to create a positive learning environment are similar regardless of the age or stage of students, for example, providing clarity in expectations, negotiating parameters and developing mutual respect (Rogers 2007).

However, the most striking difference between schools and FE is the part that the whole school ethos and culture have in underpinning approaches to behaviour management. Teachers in schools have a core professional responsibility to ensure a 'professional regard for the ethos, policies and practices of the school in which they teach' (DfE 2011), and the whole school approach to behaviour management is a central aspect of this practice and policy. Consistency in approach in schools is desirable and seen as a marker of good leadership, management and organization (Ofsted 2015; Rogers 2007). Yet for those familiar with the relative autonomy of FE, school rules and practices can often seem alien and overly precise. For example, checking dress codes at the door, duty rotations, monitoring corridors at lesson change-over and enforced whole-school consistency are not routinely observed in FE.

Such specific approaches arise from the fact that schools are fundamentally very different in their operation to FE colleges. Schools cater for students who are within a narrow age range; split most visibly by chronological age rather than level of study; and are required to follow a standard academic curriculum until GCSE in all but the most unique situations. Likewise class sizes are rarely below 25–30 students while attendance is full time and entirely supervised. Schools are therefore organized to meet the needs of young people at certain developmental stages in specific circumstances.

Table 9.1 highlights the core differences and similarities in the approach and organization of behaviour management in schools and FE and considers some of the core variations between current inspection frameworks in these areas (Ofsted 2015, 2016).

Exploring ethos in schools

Glance briefly at the website, policies or prospectus of most schools and it is difficult to avoid the words 'ethos', 'mission', 'values' and 'culture'. Artefacts of these concepts are frequently visible throughout: school badges, mottos and displays all provide a nod towards the intended ethos and culture of the school. While these artefacts and statements are useful methods of communication that act as concrete visual representations of broadly abstract concepts, they become meaningless if the ethos of the school is not reflected through lived experience. For the stated ethos to have a positive impact it must be experienced by staff and students daily and be reflected in actions, relationships and learning (Graham 2012).

The development of a positive school ethos is increasingly viewed as essential to the improvement of academic standards, social mobility and the well-being of young people (Kauffman et al. 2014). Ethos and culture are frequently identified in educational reviews as a necessary component for sustained improvement across a range of contexts, for example, in closing social and geographical attainment gaps (Ofsted 2013) or in the protection of

Table 9.1 *Behaviour management compared*

Schools	Points of intersection	Further education
• Whole school expectations are detailed with clear outcomes for non-compliance.	• The behaviour and welfare of students is an institutional responsibility.	• Students are given a high degree of personal autonomy within guided boundaries.
• Consistency between all staff within and beyond the classroom is expected.	• Creating positive attitudes to learning and progress is a core requirement.	• Whole institution guidelines are broad in their nature and adapted to specific learning environments.
• Daily routines are closely regulated both within and outside the classroom.	• Behaviour is linked to personal development and welfare in inspection frameworks.	• Behaviour policy is a 'formal' process.
• Consistency in all aspects of behaviour is required across subjects and teachers.	• Attendance is linked to the creation of a positive environment in inspection frameworks.	• Subject/local level behaviour management is core.
• Data and monitoring systems are often used to track behaviour (e.g. missed homework, low-level disruption) at classroom level.	• Students should feel safe and know who to approach for guidance and advice.	• Wider pastoral support is managed by central support services.
• Daily and/or weekly tutor time is standard.	• There is a responsibility to ensure the safety of students.	• Attendance is monitored internally; national benchmarks do not directly impact inspection judgements.
• Form tutors act as a core point of contact for their students and for staff.	• Students are expected to be educated to protect themselves from risks (internet, bullying, extremism, etc.).	• Emphasis on employment and work-based behaviours.
• Uniforms and the consistent use of planners, etc., are common.	• Behaviour is managed through both subject and pastoral systems.	• Pastoral tutor roles where they do exist are not as clearly defined.
• Contact with parents is expected for partnership relationship.	• A range of specific in-class strategies work across contexts.	• Contact with parents is limited and for younger students only.
• Behaviour is usually commented on during statutory reporting processes.	• Behaviour management, learning and progression are closely linked.	
• Key members of teaching staff take on specific responsibilities linked to multi-agency working and wider well-being.		
• All staff are required to take on significant timetabled pastoral roles.		
• Attendance is legally required with clear national thresholds.		
• Exclusion data is reportable and linked to national benchmarks.		

young people from extreme views (Ofsted 2017). Ethos appears in headlines and political speeches with regularity cited by politicians, researchers and charities as a core aspect of improvement in multiple contexts. It is also highlighted as a core foundation for effective leadership and governance (DfE 2017) and is at the heart of discussions around behaviour management (Rodgers 2015).

Yet there is a tacit assumption that we understand and consistently define what ethos and culture are. There is a presumption that we understand their parameters and can clearly identify their actualization in practice. However, ethos is a notoriously slippery concept that defies clear explanation (Allder 1993; Donnelly 2000; McLaughlin 2005). We may instinctively recognize the broad scope of the concept but creating a clear shared definition that encapsulates its full meaning within educational environments is more challenging. Ask a group of teachers what they believe ethos to be and the answers vary wildly; ask them what constitutes a positive ethos, how it is created and how it can be observed, and a lively debate ensues.

The concept of ethos becomes even vaguer when we consider its parameters, exploring how it tessellates with the equally ill-defined and pervasive terms of values, atmosphere, culture and mission. Maughlin (2005) argues that in searching for clarity in the concept of ethos, its complications should be embraced and its range of meaning and nuances explored. This is wise advice since approaches to the creation of a positive ethos should not, in practice, be prescribed as schools are so contextually varied. Likewise, maintaining conceptual range also acknowledges the subjective components of a school that cannot be measured or easily identified yet nonetheless have an impact on student experiences, outcomes and perceptions.

Yet embracing the complexity of ethos is also problematic. Without clear conceptualization, discussion and exploration of approaches, their impact can lack focus in both research and practice. Discussion can become generic and ethos and culture can become sidelined as more tangible features take precedence. This breadth in definition also results in a dearth of literature that empirically measures, critically evaluates or reflects upon the concept (Donnelly 2000). However, despite limited evidence ethos is identified as an essential element of educational policy and a vital aspect of successful school improvement with its significance widely recognized and accepted by government agencies, researchers and practitioners (Graham 2012). Indeed, it seems this is a rare point of consensus among the disparate arms of educational organization and practice.

Where research has taken place, ethos has been identified as supporting positive academic outcomes (Allder 1993), improving life chances (Rutter 1979), building culturally diverse communities (Johnson 2003) and in being central to the total quality improvement of schools (Stratford 1990). Furthermore, the promotion of a positive institutional ethos has been identified as having a positive effect on health-related outcomes and school engagement (Bonnell et al. 2007) while improving attitudes towards clusters of risky behaviours including alcohol and drug misuse, exposure to unprotected sex and low levels of school engagement (Hawe et al. 2015).

So, while there are relatively few attempts to fully explore and conceptualize ethos and culture within educational institutions (McLaughlin 2005) and without this clarity in definition empirical exploration of its impact may remain limited (Donnelly 2000). There is nonetheless enough understood about these concepts to suggest that they have become an area of increasingly defined practical focus since at present they are pervasive ideas but underutilized and sometimes poorly understood (Policy First 2010).

In many ways the same considerations could be applied within FE. However, it is arguable that while FE colleges do promote a defined ethos, its underpinning drivers are different to those of schools. On a simple level, colleges are businesses with wide-ranging operations that must be captured in their entirety by the overarching vision and corporate identity of the institution. Moreover, colleges are frequently large and the culture evident across departments can vary dramatically. This is not accidental; specific departments maintain links with different industries and in preparing vocational students for roles within specific workplaces, it is desirable to guide students towards the cultural norms they will experience in employment, for example, students following a public services route need to adopt different behaviours to those focusing on services industries. Ethos and culture in colleges then become less holistic and more specific; less linked to the development of a rounded set of fundamental behaviours and outlooks and more driven by the need to shape existing behaviours for specific work-based roles. Such an emphasis can be seen within the current Ofsted framework which emphasizes preparation for employment (Ofsted 2016). As such the holistic approach to ethos, culture and behaviour management evident in successful schools is not as visible, nor perhaps as desirable, within an FE college setting.

Ethos, culture and behaviour management

Behaviour management in schools is often viewed as an iceberg. The aspects you see enacted when disruption takes place are the most visible; it is these areas that the school behaviour policy seeks to address. This sharp end of the process also receives the greatest focus during ITE and ongoing CPD (Carter 2015). Yet much of the work of behaviour management in schools is enacted beneath this surface mitigating, through routine and consistency, the use of visible behaviour processes. Focusing on creating a positive ethos and culture within the whole school is key to giving structure and vision to this wider conception of behaviour management (Stratford 1990). This is like FE contexts but within FE the creation of this climate is grounded within the course and in ensuring wider support and academic services are accessible.

Poor standards of behaviour are widely recognized as negatively impacting learning and progress. However, simply managing behaviour is not enough in ensuring the best outcomes for all students. Instead the aim should be to actively promote behaviours and attitudes that are positive and constructive. It is here that ethos and culture are identified as enhancing outcomes (Thacker and McInerney 1992; Glover and Law 2004) and ideas that have their basis within the work of Rutter et al. (1979). Here school effectiveness was explored demonstrating that the outcomes and experience of students in some schools were more positive than expected given their context. This additional value could not be easily attributed to underlying factors, for example the student population, institutional organization, curriculum or community links. Therefore, the idea of school ethos was introduced to explain the differential; ethos was identified as the missing ingredient, the gap between contextually similar schools, whose students should be achieving the same outcomes but were not.

In the following quotation Allder (1993: 63) at once seeks to describe ethos, to reveal its complexity and to highlight the tension at its core:

> The ethos of a school, that illusive item which is so difficult to recognise, measure or improve, is the unique, pervasive atmosphere or mood of the organization which is brought about by activities or behaviour, primarily in the realm of social interaction and to a lesser extent in matters to do with the environment, of members of the school, and recognised initially on an experiential rather than a cognitive level.

Here Adler identifies a central problem, quite simply, the stated ethos of a school may be very different from that which is experienced by its staff and its students. Donnelly (2000) notes this disconnect for teachers highlighting that teachers' lived experience frequently diverges from the stated rhetorical stance of the institution, suggesting that ethos is a dynamic, multifaceted concept operating on a range of, not always harmonious, levels. A similar gap has also been noted in the relationships between students and teachers (Solvason 2005) and in the experiences of students (Graham 2012). For Graham (2012: 352) there is a detachment between stated aims and actual experience with ethos identified as a 'first-hand experience that is created by acts of solicitude'. Here ethos is linked to moods, relationships and social interaction and evolves, emerging in an organic way that is subject to change and development. Acknowledging the capacity of ethos evolves enabling negative experiences to be made positive by a consistent focus on relationship building and the promotion of a shared culture.

Focusing on shared values is also recognized as a significant factor in supporting school responses to demographic changes, including wider ethnic diversity and increased migration, by promoting culturally responsive learning environments that value diversity and meet the needs of all students (Johnson 2003). The need to create culturally aware learning environments is reflected in the practical advice available which advocates the need to clearly define and articulate a whole school vision that is visible through symbols, modelling and daily interactions that reinforce a common cultural experience (Policy First 2010).

By contrast in FE colleges the artefacts of ethos are clearly visible but the breadth of provision (from non-award-bearing courses to higher education) and the range of students (ages 14 to 80-plus) make this consistent cultural experience as much a hindrance as it is an impossibility although common values can nonetheless be promoted.

Using ethos and culture in practice to support behaviour management

In the twenty-first century it is arguable that the development of a positive school ethos has taken on a greater importance than ever before. As one pastoral lead explains:

> In our school, developing independence, resilience and guided free-thinking through our behaviour management systems rather than pure conformity to sets of school-rules is very important … Our students often deal with challenging home lives and personal concerns. On top of this they have their own academic emotions and the external pressures of exams and their futures to manage. Socially students deal with face-to-face relationships, developing a sense of their own identity and also have to manage their on-line identities … Within our school we can't legislate for every situation our pupils encounter but we can develop in our young people the confidence and skills that will help them navigate these areas and ensure that they feel safe, supported and able to challenge themselves to do their best in all situations.

While revealing the broad underlying drivers in the approach of one school this quotation also highlights the importance of the *us* and the *we* in the development of school culture and ethos. Culture and ethos are areas that should not simply be conceived and imposed; instead they must be shaped and developed within an individual school community (Stratford 1990). The characteristics of ethos and culture may vary quite dramatically and still be equally effective, but there needs to be a sense of ownership felt by all members of a school community. Achieving this may not be straightforward but there are ways to create an environment in which this can occur.

The quotation above also reveals the breadth of the areas, within and beyond school, that are linked to behaviour management. While the ability to regulate behaviour within the subject area remains a core concern for most teachers, there are additional imperatives linked to the development of positive behaviours. Effective behaviour management has an ever-increasing reach and the capacity to equip students with the tools required to approach multiple aspects of their daily lives in a confident manner. For example, the use of social media blurs the parameters of school and home behaviours while aspects of the internet present real dangers to the safety and well-being of young people at a time when government policy in the area is dated and misconceived. However, it is arguable that developing a positive culture within schools can have a positive impact beyond.

While a broad area in theory the ethos of any school is frequently distilled by its leadership into quite snappy and clear statements of intent. Ideally this stated ethos should be communicated clearly by leaders, reflected through core policies, promoted by staff through their practice and reflected in the attitudes, behaviour and outlook of its students (Figure 9.1). Such an approach should be an iterative one that enables the stated vision to

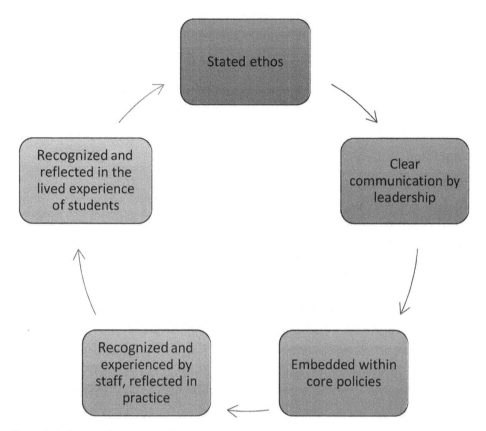

Figure 9.1 *Putting ethos into practice.*

remain stable but adaptive to changing circumstances and challenges. If a school's defined ethos is successfully reflected, it should be readily articulated by all (Allder 1993).

Such an approach is particularly important for the area of behaviour management. While learning and teaching can be successfully approached in a variety of ways across an institution, and from lesson to lesson, behaviour management needs consistency in order to thrive (Bennett 2017). The specific systems and approaches employed can vary across schools; in many ways specific strategies are less important to ensuring effective behaviour management than the way this is achieved and organized. However, clarity in communication, an understanding of responsibility and clear lines of accountability are all fundamental.

Yet frequently when discussing behaviour management, the importance of these wider structures and the day-to-day organization are overlooked while the promotion of positive behaviour takes second place to responses to negative behaviours. Trainees and newly qualified teachers in particular can have a limited awareness of how whole school structures might operate or the importance of their role within these. For new teachers, learning to act as part of a much wider team and to ask for help without feeling inadequate can be a steep learning curve (in itself, culture can go a long way to encouraging this). All too often behaviour management is addressed as a series of strategies for preventing and handling specific levels of disruption at classroom level; however, for behaviour management systems to work effectively the constituent parts require integration, and behaviour management should be clearly linked to and reflected in all aspects of core school policy (Figure 9.2).

So, what steps can schools take to create a positive ethos and ensure the application of effective behaviour management systems? The following key points can be considered as a starting point:

1 **A clear whole-school approach** that is linked to an aspirational vision for the culture of the school and reflected in all core policies.
2 **Clear communication** of the school ethos through visible symbols, discussion and a clear modelling of specific expectations.
3 **Culture created daily** through the actions and behaviours of staff and students.
4 **School and classroom routines** designed to reflect the desired culture and expected behaviours. These should be embedded and consistently applied.
5 **Recognizing** the ethos and culture of the institution as a whole and celebrating the contribution of individuals to this.
6 **CPD and training** explicitly and consistently focus on ethos, culture and behaviour management, providing opportunities for staff to share practice, foster relationships and seek support.

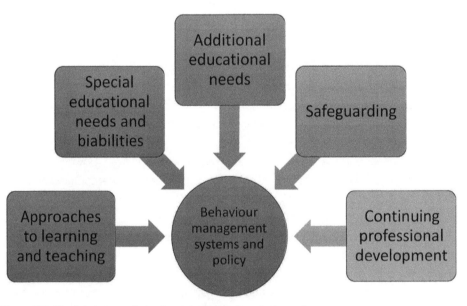

Figure 9.2 *The links between behaviour management and other policy areas.*

7 **High expectations** where an actively positive ethos, culture and approach to behaviour are pursued.

8 **The staff team** (including auxiliary staff) are consistent in their application of whole school systems both within and outside the classroom.

9 **Evaluating the ethos and culture** of the school is undertaken alongside the evaluation of data-driven outcomes. There is an open dialogue between leadership, staff, students and parents.

Conclusion: changing culture

When approached effectively, a whole school ethos is core to the development of behaviour management systems within the compulsory sector. It is an aspect of school-based practice that is in many ways distinct from the approaches visible within FE. Staff working within schools are required to support and enact the whole school vision consistently and precisely and in doing so can create an environment that ensures students feel safe, motivated and connected. The whole school approach combines disconnected facets of school policy, supports the creation of a community and encourages in students the fundamental, active behaviours needed to tackle complex situations.

Ethos has the capacity to impact varying outcomes and experiences, but it is entirely possible to actively develop the culture and ethos of a school, using this as a catalyst for wider improvement. This is not always a straightforward process and for schools in challenging circumstances it can be particularly difficult (Policy First 2010) since culture can be ingrained and embedded change can take time and tenacity. Likewise, it is also tempting to replicate borrowed models without fully appreciating the unique context of the individual institution and for an ethos and culture to be effective they need to be recognized and owned by all stakeholders. However, the ethos and culture of a school should not be overlooked in favour of a concentration of individual outcomes and is central to the practice of teachers within the organization and their holistic approach to the area of behaviour management in particular.

Activities

1 Consider the following case study. What strategies do you think could have been employed at this school to achieve this outcome?

Case study

The leadership of one outstanding secondary comprehensive school, with a high proportion of disadvantaged and special educational needs and disability (SEND) students, states on its website that the school values strong relationships and promotes an ethos of support. When asked to describe the culture of the school, teachers note its inclusivity, levels of support, relationships between staff and students and its warmth as a place to work. Students mirror this, stating they feel they can ask for help, they can be themselves, they know where to go for help and they are confident in making mistakes. Its most recent Ofsted report highlights the role of leadership in promoting a positive and supportive culture and notes that students are polite and respectful. Students have no concerns about bullying (something which is noted as a rarity by Ofsted). The report goes on to note that the ethos is clearly communicated and promoted exceptionally well.

2 Consider the following case study. What might need to be considered in this situation? Where might the obstacles be and how might these be avoided? What strategies could be employed to help the intervention school develop?

Case study

A large (2,500 plus students), outstanding, urban teaching school with an excellent reputation and wide-ranging links has been asked to provide support to a school that requires improvement within a neighbouring local authority. The intervention school has 600 students, is rural, with a high proportion of SEND and disadvantaged students, and is a significant distance from other schools.

References

Allder, M. (1993), 'The Meaning of School Ethos', *Westminster Studies in Education*, 16 (1): 59–69.

Banerjee, R., Weare, K., and Farr, W. (2014), 'Working with Social and Emotional Aspects of Learning (SEAL): Associations with School Ethos, Pupil Social Experiences, Attendance, and Attainment', *British Educational Research Journal*, 40 (4): 718–742.

Bennett, T. (2017), *Creating a Culture: Independent Review of Behaviour in Schools*, London: Asset.

Blanden, J., and Gibbons, S. (2006), *The Persistence of Poverty Across Generations: A View from Two British Cohorts*, Bristol: Policy Press.

Bonell, C., Fletcher, A., and McCambridge, J. (2007), 'Improving School Ethos May Reduce Substance Misuse and Teenage Pregnancy', *BMJ: British Medical Journal*, 334 (7594): 614.

Carter, A. (2015), *Carter Review of Initial Teacher Training (ITT)*, Department for Education. Available online: https://www.gov.uk/government/publications/initial-teacher-training-government-response-to-carter-review (accessed 4 June 2018).

Day, C., Gu, Q., and Sammons, P. (2016), 'The Impact of Leadership on Student Outcomes: How Successful School Leaders Use Transformational and Instructional Strategies to Make a Difference', *Educational Administration Quarterly*, 52 (2): 221–258.

Department for Education (2011), *Teachers' Standards*, London: Department for Education. Available online: https://www.gov.uk/government/publications/teachers-standards (accessed 4 June 2018).

Department for Education (2014), *Qualified Teacher Status (QTS) Qualify to Teach in England*, London: Department for Education. Available online: https://www.gov.uk/guidance/qualified-teacher-status-qts (accessed 10 November 2018).

Department for Education (2016), *Behaviour and Discipline in Schools – A Guide for Head Teachers and School Staff*, London: Department for Education. Available online: https://www.gov.uk/government/publications/behaviour-and-discipline-in-schools (accessed 4 June 2018).

Department for Education (2017), *Governance Handbook*, London: Department for Education. Available online: https://www.gov.uk/government/publications/governance-handbook (accessed 4 June 2018).

Department for Education (2018), 'Staffing and Employment: Advice for Schools', London: Department for Education. Available online: https://www.gov.uk/government/publications/staffing-and-employment-advice-for-schools (accessed 10 November 2018).

Department of Health and Social Care and Department for Education (2017), 'Transforming Children and Young People's Mental Health Provision: A Green Paper'. Available online: https://www.gov.uk/government/consultations/transforming-children-and-young-peoples-mental-health-provision-a-green-paper (accessed 4 June 2018).

Donnelly, C. (2000), 'In Pursuit of School Ethos', *British Journal of Educational Studies*, 48 (2): 134–154.

Garner, P., Kauffman, J., and Elliott, J.G. (2014), *The SAGE Handbook of Emotional and Behavioural Difficulties*, London: Sage.

Glover, D., and Law, S. (2004), 'Creating the Right Learning Environment: The Application of Models of Culture to Student Perceptions of Teaching and Learning in Eleven Secondary Schools', *School Effectiveness and School Improvement*, 15 (3–4): 313–336.

Graham, A. (2012), 'Revisiting School Ethos: The Student Voice', *School Leadership & Management*, 32 (4): 341–354.

Hawe, P., Bond, L., Ghali, L.M., Perry, R., Davison, C.M., Casey, D.M., and Scholz, B. (2015), 'Replication of a Whole School Ethos-Changing Intervention: Different Context, Similar Effects, Additional Insights', *BMC Public Health*, 15 (1): 265.

Johnson, L.S. (2003), 'The Diversity Imperative: Building a Culturally Responsive School Ethos', *Intercultural Education*, 14 (1): 17–30.

Kaufman, M.R., Rimal, R.N., Carrasco, M., Fajobi, O., Soko, A., Limaye, R., and Mkandawire, G. (2014), 'Using Social and Behavior Change Communication to Increase HIV Testing and Condom Use: The Malawi BRIDGE Project', *AIDS Care*, 26:sup1: S46-S49.

McKenzie, J. (2014), *Changing Education: A Sociology of Education since 1944*, London: Routledge.

McLaughlin, T. (2005), 'The Educative Importance of Ethos', *British Journal of Educational Studies*, 53 (3): 306–325.

McLaughlin, T.H. (1994), 'Values, Coherence and the School', *Cambridge Journal of Education*, 24 (3): 453–470.

Ofsted (2013), *Unseen Children Access and Achievement 20 years on*. Available online: https://www.gov.uk/government/publications/unseen-children-access-and-achievement-20-years-on (accessed 4 June 2018).

Ofsted (2015), *School Inspection Handbook from September 2015*. Available online: https://www.gov.uk/government/publications/school-inspection-handbook-from-september-2015 (accessed 4 June 2018).

Ofsted (2016), *Further Education and Skills Inspection Handbook*. Available online: https://www.gov.uk/government/publications/further-education-and-skills-inspection-handbook (accessed 4 June 2018).

Ofsted (2017), *Ofsted Annual Report 2016–17*. Available online: https://www.gov.uk/government/collections/ofsted-annual-report-201617 (accessed 4 June 2018).

Phippen, A. (2017), 'What Do We Mean by "Child Online Safety"?', in *Children's Online Behaviour and Safety*, 1–13, London: Palgrave Macmillan.

Policy First (2010), *Ethos and Culture in Schools in Challenging Circumstances*, London: Teach First. Available online: https://cdn.lkmco.org/wpcontent/uploads/policy_first_2010_final_0.pdf (accessed 4 June 2018).

Rogers, B. (2007), *Behaviour Management: A Whole-School Approach*, 2nd edn, London: Sage.

Rogers, B. (2015), *Classroom Behaviour: A Practical Guide to Effective Teaching, Behaviour Management and Colleague Support*, 4th edn, London: Sage.

Rutter, M. (1979), *Fifteen Thousand Hours: Secondary Schools and Their Effects on Children*, London: Open Books.

Rutter, M., Maughan, B., Mortimore, P. and Ouston, J. (1979), *Fifteen Thousand Hours: Secondary Schools and Their Effects on Children*, London: Open Books.

Solvason, C. (2005), 'Investigating Specialist School Ethos… or Do You Mean Culture?' *Educational Studies*, 31 (1): 85–94.

Stratford, R. (1990), 'Creating a Positive School Ethos', *Educational Psychology in Practice*, 5 (4): 183–191.

Thacker, J.L., and McInerney, W.D. (1992), 'Changing Academic Culture to Improve Student Achievement in the Elementary Schools', *ERS Spectrum*, 10 (4): 18–23.

Zych, I., Ortega-Ruiz, R., and Del Rey, R. (2015), 'Systematic Review of Theoretical Studies on Bullying and Cyberbullying: Facts, Knowledge, Prevention, and Intervention', *Aggression and Violent Behaviour*, 23: 1–21.

10 The Use of Professional Standards for Teachers and Trainers in Promoting Positive Behaviour

JOE WEARING

Introduction

Behaviour management might be the most important thing to be taught to new teachers because of how significant it is in relation to ensuring students make progress. It must engage teachers beyond just dealing with the behaviour to discover potential causes of challenging behaviour and try to reach solutions and employ strategies that are inclusive while still recognizing the need for high expectations. Behaviour management is more than ensuring a safe learning environment; it is about planning thoughtful, engaging and even inspiring sessions for students.

The Education and Training Foundation (ETF) offers twenty Professional Standards divided into three sections: Professional Values and Attributes (PVA), Professional Knowledge and Understanding (PKU) and Professional Skills (PS). It could be argued that promoting positive behaviour management fits comfortably into any of the three areas – 'positive' here meaning that the teacher considers carefully the likely challenges in behaviour and plans to minimize these. This could be in the form of using time limits to ensure pace of activities and planning short activities to maintain engagement, offering choices of task and differentiating carefully so that learners can access the material of the lesson. Positive also means the teacher projecting a positive attitude, using praise and making the learning space a welcoming environment by doing things such as meeting-and-greeting at the door and even smiling at students as they enter the classroom!

Although only explicitly mentioned once in the Professional Standards in Standard 11 (PKU), 'Manage and promote positive learner behaviour', positive behaviour management and a safe, inclusive progress-filled classroom is achieved when behaviour management is not seen in isolation but is linked to ongoing, effective application of the Professional Standards.

It is in the word 'promote' where the significance of behaviour management and links to other standards can be made. For example, Standard 5 (PVA) says, 'Value and promote equality and diversity, equality of opportunity and inclusion.' This, it could be argued, requires the management of behaviour and a safe working environment, something achieved through positive behaviour management.

Chapter structure

The chapter is divided into sections which will act as guidelines containing references to the ETF Professional Standards and how they can be applied in relation to teacher objectives to help achieve the desired behaviour from students:

1   A clear outline of purpose (of the session and course long term).
2   A link to the personal gains to be made.
3   A clear outline of what is expected (behaviourally and productively).
4   A grasp of the expected behaviour in the situation.

The chapter will now discuss each in turn and try to explore which of the Professional Standards are covered in achieving each of the four sections in a practical way. This chapter is not intended as a critique of the ETF Professional Standards but rather suggests ways that they are relevant to behaviour management in practice.

A clear outline of purpose

Identifying the purpose of the lesson is crucial and relates to motivational factors for learners. (Standard 3 (PVA) states: 'Inspire, motivate and raise aspirations through enthusiasm and knowledge.') Some learners will simply be motivated; they understand that it is important to work and to not 'get in trouble' for not working; they like learning and freely enjoy lots of different tasks and challenges. While these learners do not necessarily populate an entire class, your objective is to try to get as many of your learners as possible to this state. Clearly explaining the purpose of both an individual lesson and the course, and repeating those messages at regular and opportune moments, creates links to the work in the lesson, to the aims of the course and makes connections to the futures of the students.

This is also an excellent opportunity to offer clear and direct instruction about what will be discussed in the lesson. Reducing the 'unknown' for the students can help them become more settled and reduces stress and anxiety, leading to a more positive outlook in the lesson which, if that positivity is fostered, can result in their being successful on the course.

Reducing the 'unknown' and the potential fear that it brings is a method that can be extended. Here are two examples of how this could be done:

1 Sharing your plan of the year or scheme of work with students so they are aware of what their progress should look like and how the course will be covered.

2 Speaking positively to students who demonstrate problematic behaviour before lessons and explaining what will be contained within them can have a very positive impact on their behaviour.

Enjoyment can be projected as a bonus for students and can be linked to Standard 13 (PS): 'Motivate and inspire learners to promote achievement and develop their skills.' It can be thought of in more tangible terms and the use of 'enthusiasm and knowledge' is helpful here. The concept of projection (Delaney 2009) outlined as a negative factor can also be reversed and seen as the positive.

There are students who need help in seeing the purpose of some tasks. This is not necessarily them being rude or difficult; they, like many of us, are perhaps trying to avoid doing something. There could be a whole host of reasons for this avoidance, not least being one of self-esteem and confidence. For many students, school or college holds the same fear and trepidation and without a clear explanation as to why it is vitally important to complete work, or take an active part in a lesson, there is a significant chance that they will misbehave to avoid embarrassment or failure. Why would those anxious, self-conscious students with low self-esteem enter a situation where they fear they will fail?

It is here, then, that the links to creating a safe learning environment can clearly be made. Safety of learners is paramount and obviously not limited to physical safety; learners must feel safe to ask questions and to try things without fear of ridicule. The creation of this safe environment is the responsibility of the teacher, and there are three ways to help achieve it:

• Be consistent

• Be fair

• Follow through on the things that you say you will do.

This allows opportunities to reinforce the purpose of the session and course to those struggling with motivation and understanding (Curzon and Tummons 2013). The creation of a safe place for all learners is something that can, in part, be achieved through the clear outline and reinforcement of behavioural expectations potentially in the form of ground rules. Lemov (2015) explores this through routines leading to increased expectations, which in turn lead to the expectation of excellence from the students. Teachers should simply be interested not in managing behaviour so that a lesson is quiet and calm but in excellent outcomes and learning; the creation of high expectations of behaviour can be a part of that. Indeed, the Department for Education (DfE) looks specifically at this in its advice document *Mental Health and Behaviour in Schools,* where it outlines the links between mental health and the need for high expectations for attainment and clear policies for the management of behaviour (DfE 2016b).

The importance of consistency cannot be understated; if learners know what to expect they can align their own behaviour to your sessions. This has implications for the consistency of expectations across the institution and a new trainee's understanding of this. By consistently dealing with the negative impact some learners' behaviour has on the confidence of others to contribute or even work hard, the teacher is promoting a safe learning environment where excellence is expected.

Standard 14 (PS) – 'Plan and deliver effective learning programmes for diverse groups of learners in a safe and inclusive environment' – deals with safety but, more crucially, uses the term 'plan'. Planning sessions carefully and considering the starting points of learners is an important part of behaviour management. Use the feedback from your students to shape their learning experience; you may have to adapt your approach of the same topic to diverse groups of students in order to maintain engagement and increase progress. In formulating these different plans, behaviour of the students is being considered and planned for. It follows, then, that if all the learners are engaged and making progress then it is an inclusive classroom.

Fairness, in a behaviour management sense, is almost inseparable from consistency. This section will not discuss the need for fairness and equal opportunities in education and will instead discuss fairness in the opportunities given for learning to take place in relation to behaviour management. Some learners may get more praise than others, some learners may be asked to contribute more than others; does this mean that the teacher is not being fair? Some learners may need more support, and some may need more engagement. Fairness is more about equivalence. Learners might not get *exactly* the same in lessons, but they get equivalent and appropriate amounts of help and support.

The behaviour management policy may have some non-negotiables and they equate to fairness: 'If anyone does X then the reaction is Y' but aside from those non-negotiables there is teacher discretion; knowledge and understanding of individual learners; their challenges and needs which might result in slightly more tolerance and lenience in some cases. But non-negotiables are exactly that and need to be upheld consistently (Jones et al. 2007). This leniency (which does not relate to non-negotiables) does not mean you are being unfair but rather that you are providing an equivalent opportunity for some learners to access education for longer than 'follow the sanctions' would allow. This does not mean that the one learner is more important than the class, but rather the one should be allowed to join the class on a mutually beneficial basis for all learners. There may also come a point where the problematic behaviour of one learner requires that person's removal from the classroom, workshop or institution despite all the efforts being made to help them succeed. This does not mean that they are 'unteachable'; it means, as Tom Bennett puts it, 'a significant minority [of students] have needs that cannot be met in the conventional classroom' (2010: 125).

A teacher doing what they say they will do (Jones et al. 2007) is key to building trust and becoming a reliable figure in the eyes of a student. If learners believe that you will do what you say, then the speed at which you are perceived as a fair and consistent teacher improves. This applies to both negative and positive assertions. For example, if you say you will have feedback on a piece of writing by Friday then you need to do it for then. You must be someone the learners can rely on; if you aren't, learners are unlikely to see you as someone who cares about them or their future and, as such, they will not care about you or what you say.

This helps develop a relationship with students that is built on trust and respect as stated in Standard 6 (PVA): 'Build positive and collaborative relationships with colleagues and learners.' These positive relationships are then based on the trust that you will be fair and consistent and have explained clearly the purpose of what students are to do. Perhaps more importantly it feeds into Standard 17 (PS): 'Enable learners to take responsibility for their own learning and assessment, setting goals that stretch and challenge.' Students will find this challenging if they are unclear as to the long-term purpose of the course they are studying. Standard 17 is the aim as students are self-motivated and clear about how to achieve their aims through the assessment methods and can identify their areas for development and then make progress in those areas. There is also the requirement for teachers to use their knowledge to enable students to know what they must do to stretch their ability in order to progress. Teachers, using data, must then enable an appropriate level of challenge for each learner so that they can do what is being asked. This is a process which will be different for each learner, the differentiation of support given to enable each learner to stretch and challenge themselves and thus achieve the aim of Standard 17 is where the teacher's ability to achieve Standard 3 is further evidenced. Consequently, when students believe they can do the work and know the purpose of why they are doing it, their motivation increases while their undesirable behaviour decreases. They become proud of their work and want to keep improving and their aspirations increase. They feel a sense of 'satisfaction' (Bennett 2010: 92) in the work that they do and that the teacher has carefully planned for them.

Example

Sometimes students do not know why they behave as they do. The conversation may be something like this:

Teacher: Why did you just do that?
Student: I don't know.

There is disbelief from the teacher that someone would act intentionally but not know why they have. The student has not considered the act or the consequences of it; they have simply acted. Perhaps this has a link to a lack of foresight. These students are living in the moment and not considering the implications of their actions. Struggling to recognize that doing something disruptive will result in sanction or punishment could be extended further and applied to their study and the importance of it to their futures. This lack of future planning further emphasizes the importance of reinforcing the message of purpose.

A link to the personal gains to be made

For this you must understand students and know their aspirations, fears, limitations, strengths and starting points. By emphasizing that the task or course that you are asking them to undertake is worthwhile will help them realize their aspirations, reduce their fears, overcome their limitations, develop further strengths and further their starting points (Petty 2014). This requires gathering data in order to make those personal connections to students.

Hopefully, students have chosen the course because it will help them achieve their goal and therefore their aspirations are being partly met by the course. Realistically, with the raising of the school leaver age this may not be the case. Often vocational courses are regarded as the route for students who have not succeeded academically at school; yet this may not be the answer (Wallace 2013). If sessions are not engaging and relevant, the student is likely to see you as someone who cannot help them achieve their goal and the chances of them becoming disruptive and disengaged are increased.

How can sessions be made engaging and relevant? It is defined in Standard 4 (PVA): 'Be creative and innovative in selecting and adapting strategies to help learners to learn' and Standard 14 is also useful. Selecting relevant case studies and articles or using examples based on the interests (both personal and professional) of the students in the group can help the understanding of the relevance of the material being covered. Providing students with a choice from a range of methods of delivery and recording and submission of work can also help students have the sense that the course is designed with them in mind, and it is supporting them in achieving their own goals and ambitions.

The best-case scenario is when the students make it relevant to their personal gains themselves. Breaking down a long course into manageable chunks with clearly signposted and measured achievement and progress ideally by the students themselves is an excellent way to achieve that. Having clear and expected outcomes shaped in discussion with students (Sutton 2000) helps define to students how they will demonstrate and recognize their own progress and, in doing so, helps them focus on achievement rather than failure, which then promotes learning and reduces issues around behaviour.

Example

A student with challenging behaviour because of a volatile home life had little to no interest in school and what education could offer. He/she was often removed from classrooms after disrupting the learning of other students. Once it was discovered that this student was very interested in hairdressing, there were avenues that could be explored. A hairdressing apprenticeship was found which also contained a requirement for exam passes in various subjects. This long-term purpose and personal gains were the incentives and motivation required for this student to access lessons and become a positive force in the classroom.

A clear outline of what is expected (behaviourally and productively)

As teachers we prepare our students so that they can be successful in their future jobs (Standard 13). This isn't simply teaching the content of the course and the technique that will help them pass the exam, but how they should act and behave as well; progression could be defined in terms of progressing into the world of work and becoming more able to function successfully in different and unfamiliar social situations. This might be achieved by repeatedly outlining the expected behaviour or how to work effectively in groups, but it shouldn't stop with just the behavioural expectations. There must be a clear explanation of what the students are expected to produce in the lesson, what their learning, progress and interactions will look like.

Having your aims and objectives on the board and droning through them at the start of the lesson may be a way of doing this, but not the most effective. Objectives in themselves don't necessarily make for effective lessons; the thought, planning and resourcing are what will make a lesson effective (Standard 4 and Standard 14) but objectives can be useful in signposting progress made to learners and checking their learning throughout a lesson. This then offers the opportunity to use the different phases of lessons to explain what is expected in the next phase and how learning will be assessed (Curzon and Tummons 2013). Letting students know how to best achieve the objectives is an excellent way of supporting their progress. Successful students with clear ideas about how to progress not only in each lesson but over the course will result in fewer behaviour problems, thus creating that expectation of excellence discussed previously (Lemov 2015).

Standard 17 (PS) states: 'Enable learners to share responsibility for their own learning and assessment, setting goals that stretch and challenge.' How can students assess their own progress and learning if they do not have a clear idea of what that learning and progress is supposed to look like (Black and Wiliam 2005)? It becomes understandable that students display undesirable behaviour if they have no clear idea about why they are completing a task or indeed how to do it successfully, hence the great significance for behaviour management of providing that clarity and purpose. It also follows that if a student can self-assess they can do so continuously, meaning that they are empowered to know that they are not only doing the task correctly but making progress. This has a positive impact on the behaviour of students because of the increase in their success and confidence in the subject; they are less likely to be demotivated by the content or tasks and more likely to approach them as something they can achieve, so they are more likely to be engaged and focused as opposed to being distracted and disruptive. This further demonstrates that Standard 3 and Standard 17 are closely connected to behaviour management. Students who are successful and believe that they are making progress are much more likely to behave in a positive manner; there will be fewer instances of undesirable behaviour in those classrooms.

Example

As an English teacher I would teach *how* to write in assorted styles and not just expect my students to be able to do it. We would look at examples of writing in the form and analyse its features. We would create model responses together to share good practice as well as clarify any issues. Then we would generate ideas for their own writing in a particular form and then write in that form. This demonstrated what was expected of that form of writing, explaining what they had to do to achieve success, supporting them in being successful as well as establishing how to work collaboratively and independently. Standard 1 (PVA), 'Reflect on what works best in your teaching and learning to meet the diverse needs of learners', and Standard 10 (PKU), 'Evaluate your practice with others [in this case the learners themselves as they become more able to achieve the task of writing in a particular form] and assess its impact on learning', were certainly at play here. The dialogue allowed for lots of positive reinforcement and opportunities for learners to give feedback about the process and where they felt supported in achieving the objective. As a result, it meant that mutual respect and trust grew, and students gained the sense of achievement which led to greater engagement and motivation. This allowed for much greater opportunities for students to accurately self-assess because they were confident of the quality of work they had done. This then resulted in a productive working environment, all from a worked example.

A grasp of the expected social norms of the situation

Standard 5 (PVA), 'Value and promote social and cultural diversity, equality of opportunity and inclusion', is a significant part of the behavioural expectations that should be outlined in your workspace. Teachers must be clear about what this always means and uphold these expectations based on respect and tolerance. Again, this may need reinforcing repeatedly to students but you may have only known the students for three months and the messages that inform their behaviour have been absorbed during their previous experiences in education and socially. They will require time to consider and change that behaviour. Teachers explaining the expectations repeatedly will help to communicate the message that this is a place of tolerance; a regular reminder of the social norms and expectations of your classroom is important. This can be seen in Vizard's (2012) driving analogy: experienced drivers no longer need to think about the process of driving while inexperienced drivers must think carefully about each process. In the same vein, some poorly behaved students are on autopilot and unaware of their poor behaviour because they are so used to displaying it in that context. The challenge is to explore ways to break that habitual poor behaviour.

The reasons for this inappropriate behaviour could be a dislike of the topic/subject/ teacher, a distraction away from issues relating to ability/fear of failure, concerns about their social status/peer pressure/pack mentality and struggling with family/health/personal issues. These are just a flavour of the issues that may be contributing to the student's decision to disregard expected and accepted behaviour. It is by no means an exhaustive list and a combination of these could be at play and affecting their behaviour.

How do teachers discover why students are not following expected social norms?

- Get to know your students (Standard 6).
- Design lessons that will engage them (Standards 4 and 14).
- Support them in being successful.
- Don't take their undesirable behaviour personally.
- Make sure that you have clear expectations of what the situation demands.
- Follow through with what you say will happen when someone doesn't meet those expectations.

Forming good relationships by having familiar and trusted routines and expectations is a suitable place to begin the creation of those relationships. For the particularly hard-to-reach students you will need greater effort: seek them out to explain what you will be doing in lessons; tell them how you think they will be great at whatever it is you are doing; give them a 'special role' in the task or activity; be positive and encouraging; say hello to them in the corridor; talk to colleagues about what is most effective in engaging them, the list goes on.

No one is born knowing the expected behaviour in social situations, and we have been taught them by our parents, grandparents, siblings, friends and some are learned through observation and reflection on participation. For some, that social education is very thorough, prescriptive and specific; for others, this element is unimportant, ignored and sparing. The students who have not acquired this social behaviour should not simply be castigated for their ignorance, just as students who don't know Pythagoras' theorem shouldn't be punished for their ignorance. What we can do is try to get those learners with problematic behaviour to see that their behaviour has an impact on others. If they simply don't care that their actions are having a negative impact on those around them, then that may be an instance where removal from the class is appropriate. By raising their awareness of others as a teacher you are working towards achieving the Standards 3, 4 and 17 as well as the specific behaviour management Standard 11.

Routines and clear expectations of what situations demand can help those students not only become more successful in lessons because their behaviour will be befitting of the classroom but more likely to be successful in similar situations in life. There is a reason why schools and colleges hold mock interviews with students to help them successfully get jobs or places at university; these are unfamiliar social situations that have specific expectations and require practice.

Example

Students sometimes need help in understanding the situation and how to act within it. This could be like the conversation below:

Teacher: Please don't use that language in here.

Student: I didn't say anything, that's not even swearing!

Teacher: Maybe you didn't know that [insert expletive] was swearing and inappropriate for this situation but you do now so please don't use it again.

This set out the expectations of the situation clearly and offered the student no way to excuse their language in the future. If they use that language again then it becomes actionable and sanctionable. Let's not forget that this may be the language that students use and have heard all their lives in many social situations they have experienced so they truly do not see anything wrong with it. It may take time to break those habits but that doesn't mean that they cannot do it. The repetition of their own language back to them is often found shocking and incongruous to the student which further supports the idea that the language used is inappropriate.

Underpinning it all

Trust is a very important factor in behaviour management and is a reason why teachers new to classes often struggle with behaviour management because students don't yet trust the new teacher. This is often made worse in schools and colleges with high staff turnovers where teachers have become temporary, unpredictable figures. This trust can be gained through consistency, positivity, enthusiasm, humour, reliability, politeness, preparation, subject knowledge, being interested, being approachable and the effectiveness of your presence. Being there every day is an excellent message to students that you are in it with them and you are working hard to secure their positive futures. It shows that you care and want to see them. For some of the learners with the most challenging behaviour that is crucially important because you might be the most reliable and consistent person in their lives. By doing these things the element of Standard 16 (PS) relevant to all subjects and not just those mentioned in 16 (' … overcome individual barriers to learning') will be met.

Issues of note

1. Common set of standards across the teaching profession

The issue of a common set of standards including the Teachers' Standards and the Education and Training Foundation Standards has been often acknowledged; it would have some benefits. It would create smoother transition between schools and further education colleges (FECs) for trainee teachers as their training would have the same focus and expectations regardless of their employment. The status and regard for teachers in the school sector and the ET sector would be regarded as equivalent; understanding and appreciation of the various divergences in teaching and learning, including the management of behaviour, could be improved.

The Learning and Skills Teacher Apprenticeship is a provision which provides greater fluency to trainee teacher mobility offering teaching qualifications and progression within a college in a specific subject or vocational area. Trainees are typically employed within an institution, providing a new talent pool from vocations and employment areas who do not necessarily have access to degree awards.

2. Ofsted

Ofsted demonstrates its concern with student behaviour through its focus on career guidance and motivation as indicators of outstanding personal development, behaviour and welfare. Indeed, the Outstanding criteria for personal development, behaviour and welfare is: 'Learners understand how their education and training equip them with the behaviours and attitudes necessary for success in the future as reflected by the excellent employability skills they acquire and the achievement of relevant additional qualifications' (Ofsted 2018: 48). The mention of 'behaviours and attitudes' is precisely what has been discussed: students learning how to behave in increasingly demanding situations with teachers shaping their attitudes towards their studies to enable them to believe they can and will be successful in their future trajectories. Teachers can achieve this through a positive, consistent approach to managing behaviour in support of clearly explained purpose and assessment methods in a safe, trusting environment.

3. Legislation

Legislation related to behaviour management should also be a feature of a teacher education course. The *Use of Reasonable Force* (DfE 2013) and *Keeping Children Safe in Education* (DfE 2016a) are crucial in ensuring safe working environments and that teachers are acting within the law as well as ensuring that the manage element of Standard 11 (PKU) is achieved. This also helps to realize the significance and application of Standard 12 (PKU): 'Understand the teaching and professional role and your responsibilities.' Avoidance of potential situations that may leave trainee teachers feeling isolated or vulnerable (Parry and Taubman 2013: 6) need to be addressed, something which organizations have a responsibility in terms of the welfare of employees.

Conclusion

The professional standards are there to offer a framework of approach and practice with the focus on theoretical approaches and reflection allowing, perhaps even insisting, that teachers of all experience levels develop their approaches based on research. This, at an institutional level, might require significant investment in continuing professional development but should ultimately improve the student experience as their sessions and progress will be better planned, resourced and managed.

Recent streamlining of the standards makes the achievement and evidencing of them more effective and therefore makes them a more significant tool and one that can be used to raise the professionalism and profile of certain areas like inclusion. The change to Standard 11, 'Manage and promote positive learner behaviour', might be regarded as too broad as a standard, but it does offer greater autonomy and a variety of responses for practitioners, and as professionals this is something to be welcomed.

Activities

1   Take one of the examples given above and identify how you might apply what you have learned and experienced. How you might share this with colleagues, either in a development session or within a team meeting?

2   How could you reinforce longer term aims to improve motivation of students in your own learning environment? This may relate to career fairs or career guidance.

3   What role does the use of personal gains have on student motivation? Give examples.

4   Think of practical ways in which you can forge trusting professional relationships with your students.

References

Bennett, T. (2010), *The Behaviour Guru*, London: Continuum.

Black, P., and Wiliam, D. (2005), *Inside the Black Box: Raising Standards through Classroom Assessment*, London: Granada Learning.

Curzon, L., and Tummons, J. (2013), *Teaching in Further Education*, London: Bloomsbury Publishing.

Delaney, M. (2009), *Teaching the Unteachable: Practical Ideas Give Teachers Hope and Help when Behaviour Management Strategies Fail*, Duffield: Worth Publishing.

Department for Education (2013), *Use of Reasonable Force in Schools*. Available online: https://assets.publishing.service.gov.uk/government/uploads/system/uploads/attachment_data/file/444051/Use_of_reasonable_force_advice_Reviewed_July_2015.pdf (accessed 3 July 2018).

Department for Education (2016a), *Keeping Children Safe in Education*. Available online: https://assets.publishing.service.gov.uk/government/uploads/system/uploads/attachment_data/file/550511/Keeping_children_safe_in_education.pdf (accessed 3 July 2018).

Department for Education (2016b), *Mental Health and Behaviour in Schools*. Available online: https://assets.publishing.service.gov.uk/government/uploads/system/uploads/attachment_data/file/508847/Mental_Health_and_Behaviour_-_advice_for_Schools_160316.pdf (accessed 3 July 2018).

Jones, F.H., Jones, P., and Jones, J.L.T. (2007), *Tools for Teaching: Discipline, Instruction, Motivation*, Santa Cruz, CA: F.H. Jones & Associates.

Lemov, D. (2015), *Teach Like a Champion 2.0: 62 Techniques That Put Students on the Path to College*, San Francisco, CA: Jossey-Bass.

Ofsted (2018), *Further Education and Skills Inspection Handbook* . Available online: https://assets.publishing.service.gov.uk/government/uploads/system/uploads/attachment_data/file/696842/Further_education_and_skills_inspection_handbook_April_2018.doc.pdf (accessed 3 July 2018).

Petty, G. (2014), *Teaching Today: A Practical Guide*, Glasgow: Oxford University Press.

Parry, D., and Taubman, D. (2013), *UCU Whole College Behaviour Management: Final Report*. Available online: https://www.ucu.org.uk/media/5693/UCU-whole-college-behaviour-policy-project-report/pdf/UCU_Whole_College_Behaviour_Management_Final_Report_June_2013.pdf (accessed 3 July 2018).

Sutton, R. (2000), *Primary to Secondary: Overcoming the Muddle in the Middle,* Salford: Ruth Sutton Publications.

Wallace, S. (2013), *Managing Behaviour in the Lifelong Learning Sector*, Exeter: Learning Matters.

Vizard, D. (2012), *How to Manage Behaviour in Further Education*, London: Sage.

Index